ry,
Street,
.

How to Feed Your Family
on Less than €1

How to Feed Your Family on Less than €10 a Day

And Other Cost-Saving Tips

Elizabeth Bollard

ORPEN PRESS

Orpen Press
Lonsdale House
Avoca Ave
Blackrock
Co. Dublin
Ireland

e-mail: info@orpenpress.com
www.orpenpress.com

© Elizabeth Bollard, 2012

ISBN: 978-1-871305-49-4
ePub ISBN: 978-1-871305-67-8
Kindle ISBN: 978-1-871305-68-5

Printed in Ireland by Colorman Ltd.

Acknowledgements

I would like to dedicate this book to my mother, with gratitude for the tremendous love, generosity, and countless skills and gifts that she has consistently given me throughout my life. Even today, she remains strong and steadfast in her support and counsel.

Thanks also to my daughters for their patience with me when I remained in intensive writing mode during their entire summer holiday.

Thanks to my dearest friend Vera, who is always calm and composed, and who listens patiently and responds with soothing and uplifting advice.

Thanks to Alex, my brilliant legal consultant, who patiently answered lots of questions and explained a multitude of legal terms, while providing precious insights into the legal profession, in both civil and criminal aspects of the law.

Most especially, thanks to Elizabeth, my editor, for believing in this project and encouraging me to write.

Contents

Preface

Today, 25 April, I am skulking around the countryside using back roads, because, for the first time in my adult life, my car tax has expired and I can't afford to renew it. All my accounts – personal and business – are overdrawn to the limit, and my credit cards are at the maximum, with monthly payments overdue.

I am counting down the days to the last working day of the month when my salary appears in my bank account. Thankfully, my children will not starve, due to my account in the local co-op store, which is up to date and allows me fuel and food for up to three months on credit, combined with the modest daily takings from my music shop.

I am also in arrears with my mortgage payments. However, there is light at the end of this tunnel because the bank has finally agreed to reduce my mortgage payment for a twelve-month period, following three requests during the past two years to avail of the six-month moratorium clause in the mortgage contract. I wrote to the bank once and my solicitor wrote on two occasions. I outlined my financial situation with total honesty each and every time. I was told that I needed to be critically or terminally ill, or unemployed, to avail of the moratorium.

I am very relieved as I write this book. It seems that I have become a master at juggling bills, dealing with financial demands and communicating with corporate organisations. I am surviving, I believe, through necessity, determination and quite a degree of stubbornness; and also because of honesty – clear and direct communication with everyone from my children, friends, colleagues, suppliers and pupils, to bank managers and large corporate organisations.

I am a single mother of three girls. One is at college, one is about to sit the Junior Certificate, and the youngest is age ten.

Before the recession, I was sorted. I appeared to have everything: three holidays a year, a nice car, designer labels. It took a lot of effort to build this lifestyle and to remain comfortable. By effort I mean ripping up floor boards in old houses at 10.00 p.m. following a day's work – I had worked non-stop for years renovating houses during the property boom. Because of all of this work, I never had problems paying the bills.

My financial difficulties arose because I purchased a new home in October 2007 on the strength of a firm 'sale agreed' on the house I was living in. I felt the need for a fresh start with the girls in a new environment. It was supposed to be my final stressful ordeal; afterwards, life should have been perfect. I was already committed to purchasing the house and was ready for what should have been a comfortable lifestyle, with less working hours and more quality time with the girls. However, as things turned out, the exact opposite occurred. The couple purchasing my old house decided to go their separate ways on the exchange of contracts. So I found myself with a combined mortgage payment of €2,750 monthly, between the two houses, fixed for five years at a set percentage.

The pressure was on. I fell and broke my wrist within two weeks of moving into the new house. Seeing as I'm a professional violinist, this was an absolute catastrophe. I couldn't play or teach violin for nine weeks, and my greatly needed tuition income was cut. Because of the recession, I could not sell my house. All our luxury was abruptly curtailed – and our lifestyle had to be adjusted.

In 2009, following the announcement from my eldest daughter that she wished to do a six-year course in college, I realised that another source of income was necessary. I used borrowed money from the bank for house improvements to open a music shop on a shoestring budget. I knew this was really pushing the boat out, but it was necessary.

Since October 2007, I learned and discovered some useful and clever ways to survive, and I know that passing these methods on will help many others. I have written this book as a means of support, guidance and reference. Most importantly, I want to give hope to families in these challenging recessionary times.

I hope you will find the content beneficial.

Elizabeth Bollard
Spring 2012

How to Feed Your Family on Less than €10 a Day

Feeding my family on less than €10 a day is a skill that I developed through necessity. I am thankful for the benefits of it.

I was forced to choose healthy, fresh, nutritious ingredients for my family and to cook basic meals regularly. I learned to make my own soups, stews, roasts, cakes, cookies and breads with the simplest of ingredients. Processed foods disappeared from my kitchen cupboards and fridge. I learned that planning my meals daily helped me to budget more frugally, and less food was wasted through going off.

My Method

Shopping for Groceries

Around this time last year, I started by looking on the websites of all the biggest grocery retailers and checking my regular shopping list against them, looking for the cheapest price for each product. I discovered that, with some retailers, just special offers are flagged on their websites and it is not always possible to shop online. However, it is possible to shop online with Tesco (www.tesco.ie), and they will deliver the groceries to your door for an additional cost of €5.50.

I looked at the groceries and their prices on the Tesco website, with a self-imposed limit of €140 for a two-week stock of groceries. Armed with this information, I planned to then go to my local Tesco and purchase the items.

The Tesco website is well designed and easy to use. It gives the shopper lots of scope to 'put in' and 'take out' products, and to browse all types and brands of the same product and their prices. As you proceed, what you are spending is totted up and visible to you.

With my specific list of items, exact prices and amounts, I commenced shopping quite late, at 10.30 p.m., because I wanted to shop at a slow pace, without hustle and bustle, while checking out any other end-of-day price reductions on the shop floor.

The results were brilliant. I succeeded in getting most of the items on my list, and because I had a detailed list of the price of each item from the Tesco website, I managed to find some things even cheaper and was able to purchase some additional items. The total cost was €134.58 out of a budget of €140, and the items purchased fed a family of two adults and two children for two weeks. Of course, I needed to buy fresh milk, butter and eggs every week, so the remaining €6 went towards this cost.

I did my complete shop in one store, for convenience really, because I work. The 24-hour opening hours suit me, and I have very little time to shop in more than one location. I am aware that some of these groceries can be obtained cheaper in other stores, like Supervalu and Dunnes Stores. If you have time, do a little more price surveillance and get the cheapest price. You may end up with items from three different stores and do even better than I did.

Below is an example of one of my recent shopping lists, including weights/amounts and prices. I found it interesting to note that the same offers still exist in 2012 as did in 2011 and, while some prices did vary, the overall cost of a two-week shop had remained more-or-less the same.

Shopping List, April 2012

Product	Price
1 Tesco Value Long Grain Rice (1kg)	€1.98
1 Tesco Fresh Cream (250ml)	€1.19
1 Tesco Fast Action Dried Yeast (56g)	€0.99
1 Dr Oetker Baking Cases (100)	€0.79
1 Tesco Chocolate Dessert Sauce (300g)	€1.59
1 Lyle's Golden Syrup (454g)	€1.32
1 Tesco Caster Sugar (1kg)	€1.75
4 tins Tesco Italian Chopped Tomatoes (400g each)	€3.96
1 Odlums Self-Raising Flour (1kg)	€1.46
1 Odlums Cream Flour (1kg)	€1.46
1 Tesco Fresh Milk (2l)	€1.99
1 Tesco Butter (454g)	€2.19
2 Tesco Everyday Value Eggs (12 each)	€4.30
1 Tesco Irish Pork Chops (1300g each)	€10.00
2 MoyPark Chicken Fillets (950g each)	€10.00
1 Tesco Healthy Eating Diced Lamb (307g)	€5.49
2 Tesco Minced Beef (800g each)	€6.00
4 Tesco Everyday Value Whole Chickens (1–1.59kg each)	€11.52
1 Denny Ham (300g)	€4.99
1 Market Value Red Onions (1.5kg)	€0.89
1 Market Value Cucumber	€0.69
1 Market Value Gem Lettuce (twin pack)	€0.99
1 pack Tesco Salad Tomatoes (6)	€0.69
1 pack Market Value Baby Tomatoes (250g)	€0.95

How to Feed Your Family on Less than €10 a Day

Product	Price
1 Market Value Cabbage	€0.99
1 Tesco loose broccoli (1kg)	€1.14
1 pack Market Value Parsnips (500g)	€2.58
1 pack carrots (600g)	€0.69
1 garlic	€0.68
1 bag seasonal loose potatoes (5kg)	€1.50
1 bag loose Rooster potatoes (10kg)	€10.00
2 packs kiwis	3 for €3.00*
1 pack ripen-at-home nectarines	3 for €3.00
2 Tesco punnets of grapes	3 for €3.00
1 Tesco Goodness Pear Pack (6)	3 for €3.00
2 banana packs (10 per pack)	3 for €3.00
1 Tesco Goodness Apple Pack	3 for €3.00
2 Everyday Value Orange Packs (12 per pack)	€3.18
1 HB Vanilla Ice-cream (1l)	€2.00
1 Tesco Double Strength Orange Squash (750ml)	€2.30
1 Tesco Classic Coffee (100g)	€1.25
1 Tesco Value Roast Coffee (227g)	€1.39
1 Barry's Tea (100 bags)	€2.99
1 stock cubes (beef)	€0.99
1 stock cubes (chicken)	€0.99
1 Tesco Value Cheddar Cheese (350g)	€2.35
1 Homecook Wonderbar cooking chocolate (150g)	€0.85
1 Flahavan's Porridge Oats (1.5kg)	€2.35

Product	Price
1 Oriental and Pacific Soy Sauce (200ml)	€0.99
1 Tesco Sunflower Oil (1l)	€1.59
1 Tesco Dried Parsley (11g)	€0.54
1 Tesco Natural Sweetcorn (325g)	€0.79
1 Tesco Value Sausages (227g)	€0.79
1 Tesco Market Value Rashers (250g)	€2.48
Total:	€131.58

* Tesco offer on selected fruit and vegetables: purchase three items from a selected range and receive the products for just €1.00 each – '3 for €3.00'. If I did not buy three items then I would pay the full price. For example, the nectarines would cost €2.99, but purchased with two other selected products, they cost just €1. I bought nine packets of fruit with this offer and so spent €9.00.

You will find, when shopping for weeks 3 or 4, that you do not need to purchase the same condiments as on your first shop, as you will not have used them all up. So you should have some money left over for little treats of your choice, or additional condiments to add to your collection.

Here are some more tips to remember when shopping for food:

• Although I went to the shop to make the above purchases, I have shopped online also. I find that online shopping stops you from impulse buying; you buy just what you need and you are in total control of your spending, so there are no nasty surprises at the end when you are at the till. Getting your groceries delivered saves you valuable time and money on petrol.

- Stick to the store's own brand when it comes to tinned tomatoes and other staples. These are cheaper than 'named' brands.
- Buy the fruit and vegetables in season, as they are fresher and cheaper.
- Buy vegetables loose, rather than pre-packed, and take time to compare price per gramme or kilogramme.
- Nuts, popping corn and sunflower seeds are healthy snack choices.
- Breakfast cereals tend to be loaded with sugar and expensive; stick to oatmeal and fresh fruit for breakfast.
- Never shop on an empty stomach, as you are more likely to buy doughnuts, cakes and pies.
- Choosing food with the furthest away best-before or use-by date gives you more time in which to use it up and reduces the chance of waste. However, often products are reduced because their expiry date is that day or the following day. This can include organic fruit and vegetables. It is only worth buying these if you are able to eat them that day or the next.
- Very often, the most expensive products are kept at eye level on the supermarket shelves. Look low down and above for cheaper alternatives.
- '50 per cent extra free' is not always the case. Look at the price per kilogramme of other brands of the same product and do the maths.

- While offers like '3 for 2', 'Buy 1 get 1 free' and '50 per cent extra free' are mostly excellent buys, very occasionally they are not, because you may not get to use up the extra food before it expires. In this context, tinned produce is always a good buy.
- There are lots of bargain opportunities out there, but avail of these with extreme caution in terms of the possible repercussions for your health. Perhaps the food on offer is fatty or loaded with sugar. Also, you may be buying and eating more than you need.
- Remember to provide your own shopping bag or get a box from the store, as each plastic bag costs €0.22 and it all adds up.

You may have noticed that my shopping list does not have bread, biscuits, cakes or sweets on it, save for the chocolate which I use in my muffins and cookies.

I make my own bread, rolls, scones, muffins, cakes and biscuits (the recipes follow in Chapter 2). These are fresh, much more satisfying, nutritious and cheaper by far than shop-produced baked goods. When I began to bake, I was surprised to find that it is easy, once you measure the ingredients accurately and observe the oven temperatures. I have become fast and quite skilled at baking, which is amazing because I never before saw myself as being domesticated and I loathe housework.

Planning Meals

I plan each day's meals (including lunch boxes) in a menu format. I have learned this means little or no waste and that every item in my shopping basket will be used. My two-week menu* is laid out below.

This does not take into account school lunches: I address making healthy and attractive lunches on a budget later in this chapter. You do not need to stick exactly to this menu; you might want to interchange meals, or substitute fish for meat (fish and meat recipes follow in Chapter 2). You may like to plan your own menu.

We squeeze fresh fruit and vegetables for fresh juice at any time of day. I was given a gift of a Philips Juicer in the past year and this really is tremendous. It takes whole fruits and vegetables with their skin on, and in seconds produces fresh sugar-free juices and smoothies.

Two-Week Menu

Week 1
Day 1
Breakfast: sweet pancakes with fresh fruit
Lunch: creamy carrot soup with bread rolls

---

* Some of these items do not appear on my sample shopping list, but you will alter and adapt your own list as you spot good offers and become more confident, skilled and perhaps adventurous in the kitchen.

Dinner: roast chicken, cabbage and mash, and stuffing

Day 2
Breakfast: porridge with chopped banana and syrup
Lunch: quiche and salad
Dinner: meat loaf with mashed potato and onion sauce

Day 3
Breakfast: boiled eggs with toast
Lunch: pasties
Dinner: vegetable curry with egg fried rice

Day 4
Breakfast: muffins – plain or apple
Lunch: potato cakes with coleslaw
Dinner: pork casserole

Day 5
Breakfast: savoury pancakes
Lunch: vegetable soup
Dinner: stewed chicken and vegetables with mashed potatoes

Day 6
Breakfast: flapjacks, toast and fresh fruit
Lunch: chicken soup with fresh rolls
Dinner: pasta with Bolognese sauce

Day 7
Breakfast: scrambled eggs on toast
Lunch: pizza, garlic bread and salad
Dinner: lamb stew on a bed of rice

Week 2
Day 1
Breakfast: porridge with syrup, chopped kiwi and
  apple
Lunch: quiche with coleslaw and lettuce, garnished
  with grated carrot
Dinner: burgers with chips and French fried
  onions

Day 2
Breakfast: savoury pancakes
Lunch: baked potatoes with chopped ham
Dinner: meat sauce with creamed mashed pota-
  toes

Day 3
Breakfast: muffins with apple or chocolate chips
Lunch: cabbage soup with garlic bread
Dinner: chicken curry with fried rice

Day 4
Breakfast: fried bacon with eggs
Lunch: chicken and ham Chinese fried rice
Dinner: pan fried pork chops with baked parsnips
  and sautéed potatoes

Day 5
Breakfast: fruit kebabs and toast
Lunch: potato and onion cakes, with lettuce, tomato, red onion and coleslaw
Dinner: roast chicken with chips and French fried onion rings

Day 6
Breakfast: omelette
Lunch: vegetable soup with chicken rolls
Dinner: cottage pie with chips

Day 7
Breakfast: fried sausages, bacon, eggs and tomatoes; toast; fresh fruit
Lunch: pizza with garlic bread
Dinner: roast chicken, with roast potatoes, egg fried rice and creamed carrots

Lunch boxes

Lunch boxes for children and adults can prove a challenge daily, both on the nutrition front and also in varying the content.

A growing number of schools have taken welcome healthy initiatives and are now firmly advocating what is and is not permitted in the lunch box. Sweets, biscuits, cakes and fizzy drinks have been banned in my child's school.

So, I am faced with having to provide an attractive and nutritious lunch for my children every day. Success (with victory dance of course!) is a completely empty lunch box at the end of the day. Failure and despondency equals the lunch box that is half to two thirds full.

Carbohydrates prove to be excellent fillers and seem to satisfy the hungry scholar for longest.

Choose one item daily from each of the following four groups for good, balanced nutrition.

You will need some good quality lunch boxes, at least two per child, and two drinks containers. Drinks might include water, milk, dilutable squash and any pure fruit juice. Make the lunch the night before, and always include a small spoon and a wipe or napkin for sticky fingers.

GROUP 1 – BREAD AND CARBOHYDRATES

The obvious choice are sandwiches made from home-baked white or wholemeal bread.

Suitable fillings could include: any leftover cold meats; cream cheese; tuna with mayonnaise and grated cucumber; tuna and mayonnaise with sweet corn; chopped ham; tomato and lettuce with mayonnaise; chicken and stuffing; sliced hard-boiled egg with mayonnaise; or chopped tomato, egg and lettuce.

Possible fillings for vegetarians would be cheese (grated), cottage cheese with chives or pineapple, coleslaw, egg mayonnaise or fish.

I avoid onions in sandwiches because the aroma can be strong and it is a little unfair to inflict it on everyone else in the classroom. In addition, your child may be left alone in the playground after eating them.

A note on sandwiches: you have probably cut them every way possible in the past – in halves, quarters or triangles. Try 'swirly' sandwiches. Butter one slice of the bread, cut the crusts off and spread cream cheese or jam on it. Roll the bread into a cylinder shape. Wrap it in cling film and refrigerate. In the morning, remove the wrap, slice the cylinder in circles and put them in the lunch box. In my experience, the novelty shape adds 'yum factor' to the sandwich, especially for younger children.

Other carbohydrate options are:

- Bread rolls with any of the above fillings
- As an occasional change, wraps are always an option instead of bread, but I find these are not as good at filling the tummy.
- Scones – sweet or savoury
- Bread sticks with dip, quiche or cold pizza
- Pasta salads or cold rice salads

GROUP 2 – VEGETABLES

Chopped carrot, cucumber, cauliflower or lettuce, with a mayonnaise, hummus or Thousand Island dip (mayonnaise and ketchup mixed).

GROUP 3 – FRUIT

Some options are:

- Any piece of fresh fruit
- Pure freshly squeezed fruit juice
- Fresh puréed fruits (stewed apple or pear)
- Homemade smoothies with soya, dairy or goat's milk, low fat yoghurt and any fresh fruit

GROUP 4 – SWEETER OPTIONS (IF ALLOWED)

Homemade muffins, fairy cakes, flapjacks, cookies, apple pie or rhubarb pie are some options.

Alternative ideas for snacks may include hard boiled eggs, sausage rolls, cocktail sausages or popcorn. Be careful of sending nuts into school with your child. Check the school policy on these first, as some children have serious nut allergies.

Important tip: plan your lunches with your daily menu. Perhaps cook a little extra rice, potatoes or pasta for dinner, and hold some back and refrigerate for the next morning's lunch box. Add chopped ham, lamb or chicken, and peas, sweetcorn or diced carrot, along with seasoning, to any of these for an instant salad. Mayonnaise on the potatoes and pasta proves tasty, while sweet and sour sauce on the rice with a little chopped pineapple is delicious.

2

Useful Low-Cost Recipes

Bread and Baking

Basic White or Brown Bread

INGREDIENTS

15g dried yeast
2 tablespoons brown sugar
1 tablespoon salt
1½kg strong white or whole wheat flour
28g butter
1 egg, beaten with a pinch of salt
850ml water

METHOD

Place the yeast and 1 teaspoon of sugar in a small bowl. Heat the water to 50°C – it is important to do this because the dough will not rise if the water is at an incorrect temperature.

Whisk 300ml of water into the yeast and sugar mixture and leave it in a warm place for 10 to 15 minutes (the oven at a low temperature will suffice) until the surface is covered with bubbles.

Add the salt and remaining sugar to the rest of the warm water for mixing with the dry ingredients.

There are two ways of doing the dough mixing; either one will do:

1. Put the flour into a large mixing bowl and rub in the butter. Pour in both the salt water and the yeast liquid. Quickly mix with your fingertips to form dough. If the dough seems too dry, add a little more water. Knead the dough for five minutes, until it is smooth, pulling the outside dough into the centre.

2. If you have a mixer, put the flour into the mixing bowl with the butter, salt water and yeast liquid. Mix this on a slow speed using the special dough hook, until all liquid is absorbed.

Continue mixing for a further two minutes.

Put the kneaded dough into a greased mixing bowl and cover it with a damp cloth. Leave it in a warm place for about 45 minutes (again, the oven on a low setting will suffice here).

The dough should double in size.

Turn it out onto a floured work surface and knead lightly, using as little flour as possible. The dough is now ready for shaping.

At this point you may choose to have 2 loaves or 40 bread rolls, or 1 loaf or 20 bread rolls.

Loaves

For the loaves, divide the dough in half. Keeping one half warm, knead the other into a smooth ball, and punch it into a 1kg loaf tin (warmed and greased); then repeat with the other half.

Brush them both with beaten egg, cover with cling film and put them in a warm, draught-free place. Leave these to further rise, until the dough reaches the top of the tin (about 20 minutes).

Bake in an oven preheated to 230°C/450°F for 20 minutes; then reduce the heat to 200°C/400°F for a further 20 minutes.

Tip the loaves out of the tins and tap the bottom. The loaves should sound hollow if cooked. Leave to cool on a wire rack.

Bread Rolls

Divide the dough into 50g portions, and roll into balls on a floured surface until round and smooth.

Arrange on a greased baking sheet and brush with beaten egg.

Cover with cling film and leave to rise for 10 to 15 minutes.

Bake at 230°C/450°F for 10 to 15 minutes.

Bread Sticks

Form small 15g portions and roll into lengths of roughly 8 inches.

You can roll these on grated cheese, dried onion granules or sesame seeds.

Bake for 5 to 10 minutes at 230°C/450°F.

Garlic Bread

INGREDIENTS

Your freshly baked bread shaped into a long roll
175g of butter, softened
2 cloves of garlic, crushed
1 tablespoon of parsley (freshly chopped is best,
but dried will do)
Salt and pepper

METHOD

Make diagonal cuts into the roll, three quarters of the way through and 1 inch apart.

Cream the butter, garlic, parsley, and salt and pepper together until thoroughly mixed.

Spread this between the cuts on the roll, and spread any remaining over the top.

Wrap in foil and bake at 200°C/400°F for ten minutes.

Open the foil and expose the top of the roll for a further 5 to 10 minutes until crisp.

Cut through each slice and serve with pizza, pasta, soup or stew.

Scones

INGREDIENTS

225g self-raising flour
½ teaspoon salt
50g butter
150ml milk
Extra milk for brushing

METHOD

Preheat oven to 230°C/450°F.

Sift the flour and salt into a bowl. Rub in the butter finely, and add the milk.

Mix to a soft dough using a knife.

Put onto a lightly floured board and knead fast until smooth.

Roll out to 1cm or ½ inch thick, and cut out 9 to 12 rounds using a cutter. The top of a glass or a cup (floured) will do if you do not have cutters.

Place on a lightly buttered baking sheet, brush with milk and bake in the oven for 7 to 12 minutes.

Cool on a wire rack, and serve with freshly whipped cream or butter.

Cheese Scones

Make as above, and throw in 60g of grated cheese prior to adding the milk.

Ham and Parsley Scones

Make as above, and add 25g of chopped ham and a teaspoon of parsley prior to adding the milk.

Tea Scones

INGREDIENTS

225g self-raising flour
½ teaspoon salt
50g butter
25g caster sugar
150ml milk
Extra milk for brushing

METHOD

Preheat oven to 230°C/450°F.

Sift the flour and the salt into a bowl. Rub in the butter.

Stir in the sugar. Add the milk and, using a knife, mix to a soft dough.

Put onto a floured surface and knead quickly until smooth. Roll out to 1cm or ½ inch thick, and cut into 9 to 12 rounds, using 6cm or 2½ inch cookie cutters.

Put onto a lightly buttered baking sheet and brush with milk.

Bake for 7 to 10 minutes.

Fruity Scones

Add in 25–50g of sultanas or currants prior to adding the milk.

Orange and/or Cherry Scones

Add in ½ teaspoon of finely grated orange rind, and/or 40g of finely chopped glace cherries, before adding the milk.

Honey Scones

Add one tablespoon of honey with the milk.

Flapjacks

INGREDIENTS

75g golden syrup
100g butter
75g brown sugar
225g oatflakes

METHOD

Preheat oven to 180°C/350°F.

Place the sugar, syrup and butter in a saucepan, and heat gently until melted. Stir in the oats and mix together.

Spread the mixture onto a greased roll tin. Smooth the top with a knife and bake in the oven for 25–30 minutes.

Leave to cool, and cut into squares.

I sometimes add some chopped almonds, coconut or really finely chopped glace cherries to the oatflakes. Dried fruits like chopped dates or apricots may be added. Currants and raisins are an option also.

Fairy Cakes/Butterfly Cakes

INGREDIENTS

100g butter, softened
100g caster sugar
2 eggs
100g self-raising flour
200ml fresh whipped cream for tops of cakes

METHOD

Preheat oven to 190°C/375°F.

Cream butter and sugar together until light and fluffy.

Beat in the eggs one at a time, adding a tablespoon of flour with each.

Fold in the remaining flour.

Put in 18 small baking cases on a baking sheet and bake in the oven for 20 to 25 minutes.

When the cakes have cooled, slice off the tops and cut them into two equal halves.

Place a dollop of freshly whipped cream on each cake, and stand the tops like butterfly wings thereon.

For a sweeter treat, put a teaspoon of caster sugar into the cream as you whip it.

Chocolate Chip Cakes

Make as above, adding 50g of chopped plain chocolate after folding in the remaining flour.

Glendine Muffins

This recipe came from my good friends Mari and Mike Hanly of Glendine B&B in Clonakilty (www.glendine.com).

DRY INGREDIENTS

315g self-raising flour
250g ordinary sugar

WET INGREDIENTS

2 medium eggs
180ml milk
60ml vegetable oil
60g butter (gently melted and cooled)

400g rhubarb (diced into small pieces)

METHOD

Preheat oven to 180°C/360°F.

Mix the dry ingredients together.

Mix the wet ingredients together.

Pour the wet ingredients into the bowl with the dry ingredients and combine gently with a dessert spoon until the mixture appears curdled.

Do not overbeat.

Fold in rhubarb – it will appear that you have too much fruit for the mixture but you will need it all.

Divide between approximately 15 muffin cases.

Fill nearly to the top of each case.

Place into the oven for 18 minutes and then, if you have two trays of muffins, swap them between the shelves for a further 8 minutes (total of 26 minutes baking).

Basic Cookies

INGREDIENTS

225g self-raising flour
1 pinch salt
150g butter
100g caster sugar
1 egg, beaten

METHOD

Preheat oven to 180°C/350°F.

Sift flour and salt into a mixing bowl. Rub in the butter finely.

Stir in the sugar. Add the egg and mix to a stiff dough.

Turn onto a floured surface and knead gently until smooth. Put in a plastic bag and chill for 30 minutes.

Roll out the dough fairly thin. Using a 5cm biscuit cutter, cut out about 30 rounds (cut roughly with a knife into shapes if you don't have a cutter).

Prick all over with a fork, and bake in the oven for 12 to 15 minutes.

IMPORTANT: leave on the baking sheet to cool.

Other Types of Cookies

Almond Cookies – add 50g of ground almonds with the sugar.

Cherry Cookies – add 50g of finely chopped glacé cherries with the sugar.

Jam Sandwich Cookies – when cold, sandwich pairs of biscuits together with jam.

Lemon Cookies – add in one teaspoon of grated lemon rind with the sugar.

Chocolate Chip Cookies – add in 50g of grated plain chocolate with the sugar.

Breakfast

French Toast

INGREDIENTS

4 eggs
1 teaspoon salt
300ml milk
10–12 slices of bread
Maple syrup or honey

METHOD

Heat a pan with a little oil.

Beat the eggs, salt and milk together in a bowl.

Immerse each slice of bread in the mix until it is well coated and has absorbed some of the mix.

Place each slice on the pan and, when the underside is browned, turn over.

When browned on both sides, serve with maple syrup or honey.

Omelette

INGREDIENTS

3–4 eggs
4 teaspoons water
Salt and pepper
25g butter

METHOD

Beat the eggs, water, and salt and pepper together.

Melt the butter in a frying pan until sizzling, being careful not to allow it to brown.

Pour in the mixture and cook for 5–8 seconds.

Move the edges with a fish slice or spatula.

Keep moving the liquid to the edges and cook for roughly five minutes or until underneath is softly firm and the top slightly moist. Fold in half and serve.

You might like to add chopped ham, onion, chopped bacon, grated cheese or chopped cherry tomatoes to the mix before pouring it into the pan.

Basic Pancakes

INGREDIENTS

285g plain flour
1 teaspoon salt
3 tablespoons caster sugar*
225ml milk
3 eggs
55g butter or 2 tablespoons oil, to fry batter

METHOD

Sift flour, salt and sugar into a bowl. Put the milk and eggs into the bowl. Mix thoroughly.

Heat pan and place the butter or oil on it.

When the butter is melted, pour on the desired amount of batter (3 to 4 tablespoons), depending on size required.

When small bubbles appear, turn it.

When the pancake is golden brown, serve with maple syrup, chocolate sauce, sugar and lemon, or chopped banana, blueberries, kiwi or any other fruit.

Serves 4.

---

* Omit the sugar in the batter recipe for savoury pancakes.

Ham and Cheese Pancakes

Grate some cheddar cheese and chop a slice of ham.

Mix and roll into prepared pancakes.

Tomato, Ham and Garlic Pancakes

Crush 1 clove of garlic and fry gently for 30 seconds in a knob of butter.

Add finely chopped tomatoes and a chopped slice of ham.

Spoon out the mixture onto prepared pancakes.

Egg, Cheese and Onion Pancakes

Take some grated cheese, a chopped hard-boiled egg and a finely chopped red onion. Spoon onto prepared pancakes.

Soups

Carrot Soup

INGREDIENTS

25g butter
1 onion – grated
225g carrots grated
1 big potato grated
25g rice
450ml water
300ml milk
½ teaspoon salt
Pinch of nutmeg
Dessert spoon of lemon juice

METHOD

Melt the butter in a big saucepan.

Add the carrot, onion and potato, and fry on a low heat for 4 to 5 minutes.

Add all remaining ingredients (save for the lemon juice) and cover and simmer for 45 minutes.

Stir in the lemon juice and serve.

Cabbage Soup

INGREDIENTS

Half a medium to large cabbage (shredded and
core removed)
25g butter
1 medium onion grated
1 clove of garlic, finely crushed
600ml beef stock
Salt and pepper
A small amount of freshly whipped cream
to garnish

METHOD

Melt the butter in a big saucepan.

Add the onion and garlic, and fry gently until soft
and golden in colour.

Stir in the cabbage and stock, and bring to the
boil. Add in salt and pepper to taste, cover the
pot and simmer for 15 minutes.

Serve with a little cream.

If you have broccoli, kale or leeks left over, add
them with the cabbage to the pan.

Vegetable Soup

INGREDIENTS

Approximately 500g of any vegetables you
choose, chopped and washed
25g butter
2 cloves of garlic, crushed
900ml water
1 to 1½ teaspoons salt
1 teaspoon parsley to garnish

METHOD

Melt the butter in a big saucepan.

Add the vegetables and cover. Leave to 'sweat' for
about 7 minutes, while shaking the pan periodi-
cally. Be careful not to let them burn.

Add the water and the salt, and bring to the boil.
Lower the heat and simmer for one hour.

The soup is equally satisfying, whether you
blend it or not. Using different vegetables each
time keeps things interesting. Stick to vegetables in season, as these are fresher and cheaper.
Using frozen vegetables is also an option – as
these are very cheap at times and may well be on
special offer.

Lamb Broth

Hold back any stock from your lamb stew, skimming off the fat on top. Throw in a handful of pasta, and simmer for a further 20 minutes. This makes a quick nutritious broth, which can be easily reheated the following day for lunch.

Chicken and Vegetable Soup

INGREDIENTS

The stock (carcass and bones removed) and vegetables remaining from your stewed chicken, with any fat on top removed (approximately 1.5 litres)
1 tablespoon flour
25g butter
Any bits of remaining chicken cut from
the carcass
1 chicken stock cube

METHOD

Add a chicken stock cube to the stock in the saucepan and simmer for a further 20 minutes.

Cream the flour and the butter together, add to the stock with the chicken pieces and let simmer for a further 15 minutes.

Blend and serve.

Steamed Dumplings

These are tasty additions to any broth. Add just before serving.

INGREDIENTS

500g plain flour
300ml water

Filling
440–500g minced chicken or pork (cooked)
2 teaspoons sugar
2 teaspoons soy sauce
spring onions, finely chopped
2 tablespoons dry sherry
3 slices fresh root ginger
2 tablespoons broth
1 teaspoon sesame oil

METHOD

Combine all the ingredients for the filling and mix together.

Sift the flour into a bowl and add the water.

Mix it well to form a dough and knead for about 5 minutes. Leave to stand for 10 minutes covered.

Remove from the bowl, cut in half and make a long roll with each piece.

Cut each into about 16 slices and roll each slice into a small ball.

At this point, spoon the filling into each one, pulling in the edges and twisting the top to seal it in.

Steam the dumplings in a steamer for 20 minutes.

Meat Main Courses

Spare Ribs with Barbecue Sauce

INGREDIENTS

10–12 single pork ribs
1 clove garlic
1 tablespoon honey
1 tablespoon dry sherry
4 tablespoons soya sauce
1 tablespoon tomato ketchup

METHOD

Oven roast the ribs at 180°C/350°F for 45 minutes.

Remove the juices and replace the ribs on the tray.

Mix together the other ingredients to form the sauce.

Coat the ribs in the sauce and leave to marinate for 1–2 hours.

Cook in the oven for a further 25 minutes.

The ribs can also be marinated in your fridge overnight, in preparation for a dinner or lunch the next day.

Stewed Chicken, Beef or Lamb

INGREDIENTS

2 medium onions
2 cloves garlic, crushed
320g selection of vegetables of your choice
25g butter
2 tablespoons flour, seasoned with salt and pepper
750ml to 1 litre water
1 stock cube (optional)
1 tin of tomatoes (optional)

METHOD

Melt the butter in a large pot, add the onions and garlic, and leave to fry gently.

Toss the meat into the flour and add to the pot. Continue to fry until browned.

Add the vegetables, and water and stock cube, and simmer over a low heat for one hour.

Meat Loaf

INGREDIENTS

500g minced beef or pork
2 tablespoons dried or chopped fresh parsley
1 tablespoon minced onion
2 tablespoons breadcrumbs
1 egg, beaten
15g butter, melted
Salt and pepper to taste

METHOD

Combine all the ingredients well together in a large bowl.

Place the mixture into a loaf tin, greased well, and cover lightly with greaseproof paper.

Bake at 150°C/300°F in a pre-heated oven for one hour.

Serve with creamy mashed potatoes, any green vegetables and gravy.

Curry – Chicken, Beef, Lamb or King Prawn

The quickest method I know is by using McDonnells Curry Powder. I love the flavour, and I can have a curry prepared in minutes. If you have more time on your hands and a more comprehensive selection of condiments, look at my curry-from-scratch recipe in the Vegetarian Main Courses section below.

INGREDIENTS

500g chicken fillets, beef pieces or lamb pieces
2 medium onions
2 tablespoons cooking oil for frying
1 tin of McDonnells Curry Powder
1 litre water

METHOD

Cut meat into thin shreds and slice the onions into 8 segments. Heat the oil in a wok or frying pan.

Add the onion and fry until soft. Add the meat and fry for 6 to 8 minutes.

Mix half of a tin of the curry powder with some of the water to make a paste.

Pour the remaining water into the pan, add the paste and stir.

When it thickens, the curry is prepared.

Serve with boiled rice, fried rice or chips.

Roast Chicken and Stuffing

INGREDIENTS

1 medium-sized chicken
6 to 8 slices of day-old bread and crumb
1 tablespoon dried or fresh thyme
1 onion, finely chopped
50g butter, cut into small bits

METHOD

Preheat the oven to 230°C/450°F.

Rinse the chicken in cold water inside and out, and place in a covered roasting or casserole dish.

Place in the middle of the oven and cook for 15 minutes. Turn the oven heat down to 200°C/390°F and cook for a further hour.

Remove the cover and cook for a further 15 to 20 minutes to brown it beautifully.

Mix all ingredients for the stuffing together, place in an ovenproof tin (I use a loaf tin), cover with tin foil and place in the oven for 30 minutes. I normally put this in the oven for the last half hour of the roasting time for the chicken without adjusting the oven temperature.

Pork Casserole with Apple

INGREDIENTS

2 tablespoons cooking oil
4–6 pork chops or 400g pork pieces
2 medium cooking apples, peeled, cored
and sliced
1 clove garlic, crushed
150ml apple juice
1kg potatoes, peeled and sliced

METHOD

Preheat the oven to 160°C/320°F.

Pan fry the pork until browned all over in the oil.

Place in a casserole dish, add the garlic, and cover with the chopped apple and onion. Add some salt and pepper.

Pour in the apple juice and cover with the sliced potatoes.

Divide the butter into little portions and place randomly on top.

Cover and cook for 90 minutes.

Uncover and cook for a further 30 minutes to brown the top.

Burgers

INGREDIENTS

750g minced beef
1 large onion, finely chopped
Salt and pepper

METHOD

Mix the beef, onion, pepper and salt to taste in a large bowl until thoroughly combined.

Divide into 7 portions and shape each into a flat round about two centimetres thick.

Cook under a hot grill for three minutes each side, or until meat is browned inside and out.

Serve with mash or chips and onion gravy (see below).

Onion Gravy

INGREDIENTS

2 large onions, thinly sliced
2 tablespoons cooking oil
1 beef stock cube
2 teaspoons plain flour
1 mug boiling water

Method

Fry the onions in the oil.

Pour in the mug of boiling water and add the stock cube and the two teaspoons of flour.

Simmer gently until thickened.

Minced Beef and Kidney Pie

INGREDIENTS

Pastry
200g flour
100g butter
Pinch of salt
A little water
1 egg, beaten/milk

Filling
400g minced beef
1 onion, finely chopped
¼lb ox kidney, chopped and trimmed
1 teaspoon gravy mix
1 teaspoon corn flour
400ml water
Salt and pepper

METHOD

For the pastry, rub together the flour, salt and butter to breadcrumb consistency.

Make a well in the centre and carefully add water, just enough to make a dough.

Knead very little, divide in half, and roll out on a floured board.

Line a greased pie dish with half of the pastry.

For the filling, fry the chopped onion in a little oil until soft.

Add the mince and kidney and fry until well browned.

Add 400ml of water with the gravy mix and salt and pepper. Cover and simmer for one hour.

Add the corn flour and stir until thick. Add more corn flour if mixture is too thin and water if it is too thick.

Once cool, spoon the filling into your prepared pie case.

Cover with the remaining pastry, paint the top with beaten egg or milk and cook in a preheated oven at 180°C/350°F for 20 to 25 minutes.

Chicken and Mushroom Pie

INGREDIENTS

See ingredients for pastry in the previous recipe
400g minced chicken fillet
50g chopped mushrooms
1 chopped onion
Cooking oil

METHOD

See method for making the pastry in the previous recipe.

Fry the ingredients for the filling in the oil.

Make a quantity of white sauce (see Sauces section later).

Add to the chicken and mushroom cooked mix.

Once filling is cool, spoon it into the prepared pie case, cover with the remaining pastry and cook in a preheated oven at 180°C/350°F for 20 to 25 minutes.

The following two recipes are for traditional dishes – **Dublin Coddle** and **Tripe and Drisheen** from Cork.

These two dishes featured in my childhood. My father hailed from Dublin and my mother from Cork, both inner-city people. Your children might not appreciate them, but if you are feeling adventurous and a little curious, try them yourself.

Dublin Coddle

INGREDIENTS

454g sausages
6 to 8 rashers
1 onion
1 litre water
Salt and pepper

METHOD

Put all ingredients in a pot and bring to the boil.

Cover and simmer for 30 minutes.

Serve over mashed potatoes.

Cork Tripe and Drisheen

INGREDIENTS

1lb tripe and drisheen*
2 onions
600ml milk
3 slices bread crumbed
25g butter
Salt and pepper

METHOD

Cut the tripe and the onions into small pieces
(I like to cut these really small, but I hear of
versions of this recipe with larger cuts). Bring to
the boil in the water with a little salt.

Simmer for 30 minutes.

Strain the tripe and onions, discard the water,
and put the tripe and onions back into the pot.

Add the milk, the breadcrumbs, salt and pepper,
and sliced drisheen, and slowly bring back to the
boil.

When the drisheen has just about changed
shape and the butter has melted, it is cooked.

Serve over creamy mashed potatoes.

---

* I favour the English Market in Cork City for this.

Fish Main Courses

Pan Fried Fish or Fish Goujons

INGREDIENTS

1kg of any type of fish, cut in strips or filleted
1 egg, beaten
300g breadcrumbs, seasoned
120g flour, seasoned
Oil for frying

METHOD

Dip the fish portions in flour and then into the egg.

Roll in the breadcrumbs and place on a hot frying pan.

Fry for about 4 minutes on each side.

Serve with wedge chips or freshly baked bread.

Fish Cakes

INGREDIENTS

12oz fish fillet, cooked and flaked
750g mashed potatoes
15g melted butter
Salt and pepper
1 egg, beaten
1 teaspoon chopped parsley
Oil for frying

METHOD

Mix the fish with the mashed potatoes, butter, and salt and pepper to taste.

Add the egg and parsley and beat well.

Divide the mixture into 8, roll into balls and flatten into cakes.

Fry on a hot sizzling pan until golden brown, 3–4 minutes on each side.

Drain and serve.

Fish Pie

INGREDIENTS

500g potatoes, cooked and mashed
Milk
50g grated cheese
1 egg yolk
Salt and pepper
Dry mustard
225g of cod, haddock or coley fillet, cooked and
flaked
1 cup parsley sauce
Pinch of nutmeg
15g butter

METHOD

Preheat oven to 180°C/350°F.

Heat the potatoes in a pot, with enough milk to moisten.

Add in half of the cheese, the egg yolk, the salt and pepper, and mustard to taste.

Put two thirds of the mixture into a buttered casserole dish.

Mix the fish with the parsley sauce, season with nutmeg and put in the centre of the dish.

Cover with the remaining mixture and decorate with a fork.

Sprinkle the rest of the cheese on top, and dot with butter.

Bake in the oven for 30 minutes.

Vegetarian Main Courses

Vegetable Curry from Scratch

Ingredients

1 tablespoon turmeric (careful – turmeric is
lethal for staining)
1 tablespoon flour
1kg of any chopped vegetables
4 tablespoons vegetable oil
2 large onions, chopped
2 cooking apples – peeled, cored and chopped
2 tablespoons curry powder
1 400g tin of tomatoes

Method

Mix together the flour and turmeric.

Put in the vegetables and toss.

Heat the oil on a frying pan, and fry the vegetables for 3–4 minutes.*

Remove them from the pan and place in a bowl.

Place the onion and the apple on the pan and fry for 5 minutes. Stir in the curry powder and continue frying.

After 2–3 minutes, pour in the tomatoes. Add the vegetables and bring to the boil.

Simmer for up to a half hour, until vegetables are cooked. Add water if it appears too thick.

Serve on a bed of boiled or fried rice, or with chips.

For **chicken, lamb or beef curry**, chop the meat into small pieces and toss in the flour and turmeric mix. Fry for up to 20 minutes until browned and cooked through. Then continue the method from * (above).

Pizza

INGREDIENTS

Base
225g strong white flour
½ teaspoon salt
7g dried yeast
1 tablespoon vegetable oil
150ml warm water
½ teaspoon sugar

Topping
400g tinned tomatoes
2 tablespoons tomato purée
Any mix of the following toppings: chopped peppers, mushrooms, red onion, pineapple, sweet corn or olives
90g grated cheese

METHOD

Sieve the flour and salt together.

Dissolve the yeast and the sugar in some of the warm water and leave in a warm place for 10 minutes.

Add to the flour with the remaining water and the oil, and mix to a smooth dough.

Flour your hands and the work surface. Knead the dough until soft, smooth and elastic. Cup your hand and make a ball of dough. Divide the ball of dough into four smaller balls, each one approximately 6cm in diameter.

Roll thinly into four 15cm circles. (You may choose to make just one pizza with all the dough if you have not got lots of time.)

Pinch the edges up and place on a baking sheet in a warm place to rise while you prepare the topping.

To stuff the crust, place grated cheese along the pinched edge and fold the edge inwards, dampening it to seal the cheese in.

Preheat the oven to 220°C/430°F.

Mix together the tinned tomatoes and the purée.

Spread evenly on the base.

Sprinkle thereon your choice of toppings.

Cover with the grated cheese. I normally use mozzarella but any cheese is fine.

Bake in your oven for 15 to 20 minutes until the crust is golden brown.

For **meat-based toppings**, choose: chopped sliced ham, chopped bacon, sliced cooked sausage, or leftover cooked chicken, lamb or mince.

Quiche

Ingredients

½ quantity of pie pastry*
Salt and pepper
230g grated cheese
2 eggs, beaten
1 onion, finely chopped
150g cooked potato, finely diced
2 regular tomatoes, finely chopped (soak in boiling water to remove skins)

Method

Preheat oven to 230°C/450°F.

Line a shallow cake tin with the pastry.

Beat the eggs and half of the cheese.

Fry the chopped onions, tomatoes and potato in butter or olive oil.

Add the fried ingredients to the egg and cheese mixture.

Spread the entire mixture on the pastry base evenly.

Sprinkle the top with the remaining grated cheese.

---

* See recipe for Minced Beef and Kidney Pie above.

Place in the oven for approximately 15 to 20 minutes, or until all cheese on top has melted and the filling has set.

For **meat-based quiches**, you might like to add some thinly sliced cooked sausage with crushed garlic. Sometimes I vary the quiche by adding a cupful of cooked rice with browned minced beef.

Side Dishes

Roast Potatoes

INGREDIENTS

750g cooked potatoes, quartered or halved
(depending on size)
Salt
50g butter
2 teaspoons olive or vegetable oil

METHOD

Preheat oven to 200°C/400°F.

Heat the butter and oil in a roasting pan.

Add the potatoes and coat well in the liquid.

Place on a tray and roast in the oven for 45 minutes.

Creamed Potatoes

INGREDIENTS

750g potatoes
Salt and pepper
40g butter
3 tablespoons milk

METHOD

Peel, wash and then cook the potatoes in salted water until tender.

Drain well and return to the saucepan.

Mash finely with a fork or potato masher.

Add the butter, milk, and salt and pepper to taste.

Other Ways of Cooking Potatoes

Sautéed Potatoes: peel, wash and remove eyes. Slice thinly and fry gently in oil, or 25g of butter.

Oven Chips: peel, remove any 'eyes' and wash and dry the potatoes. Cut each potato into 8 wedges and place on a baking tray. Brush with oil. Place in a preheated oven for 35–40 minutes until golden, turning occasionally.

Regular Chips: prepare as for oven chips, and fry in hot oil until golden brown.

CAUTION: never leave a pan or pot with oil unattended.

Baked Parsnips and Red Onions

INGREDIENTS

4 medium parsnips (or carrots), halved
lengthways
4 red onions, quartered
50g butter, melted
½ teaspoon salt
150ml water
Chopped parsley

METHOD

Preheat oven to 190°C/375°F.

Arrange the vegetables on a baking tray, coat with butter and sprinkle with the salt.

Pour the water into the dish and cover with a lid or tin foil.

Bake in the oven for 45 minutes or until tender.

Sprinkle with parsley and serve.

French Fried Onion Rings

INGREDIENTS

150g self-raising flour
Salt and pepper
4 medium onions, cut in rings
250ml cold milk
Oil for deep frying

METHOD

Season the flour with salt and pepper.

Dip the onion rings into the milk and then coat with flour.

Deep fry in hot oil until crisp and golden.

Drain on a kitchen towel and serve.

Potato and Onion Cakes

INGREDIENTS

230g self-raising flour
Pinch of salt
1 teaspoon dry mustard
100g butter
1 small onion, peeled and grated
1 large potato, peeled and grated
2 tablespoons chopped parsley
60g cheddar cheese, grated
1 egg
2 tablespoons milk
Vegetable oil for frying

METHOD

Sift flour, mustard and salt into a bowl. Rub in the butter until of breadcrumb consistency.

Add the grated onion, potato, parsley and cheese, and mix to a stiff dough with the egg and the milk.

Knead on a floured surface.

Roll the dough into a circle or square about 1.5cm to 2cm thick.

Cut into 8 portions and fry on a hot heavy frying pan, thinly coated with oil, for 2 to 3 minutes on each side.

Egg Fried Rice

INGREDIENTS

380g cooked long grain rice
1 egg, beaten
Soy sauce (1–2 teaspoons)
Salt and pepper
2 tablespoons oil for frying

METHOD

Heat the oil on a frying pan or wok. Then add the egg and scramble.

When egg is softly firm, add the rice, salt and pepper, and soy sauce.

Continue to move the ingredients around the pan until the rice is golden brown.

For **chicken, beef or lamb fried rice**, cut the meat into fine shreds and cook in the hot oil with a chopped onion (chopped garlic optional) and a handful of frozen peas until cooked through. Add the egg, and then the rice and soy sauce.

Pasta

For many years, I was intrigued by pasta, both dried and fresh. I thought that it was a highly complex recipe and art, and that only expert chefs could make it fresh (the Holy Grail!).

I went exploring lots of cookbooks and internet recipes, and I found that there was quite a variety. Some swear by using olive oil; others use milk.

I wanted authentic Italian pasta. Feeling enthusiastic, I began to look for a pasta-making gadget, and I found one. Inside the instruction book of the Italian gadget was the Holy Grail – a recipe for authentic fresh pasta.

This gadget cost me about €60, and it makes all sorts of pasta shapes, from spaghetti to lasagne sheets, and many in between.

The most interesting recommended ingredient is 00 flour. No, this is not a typo. 00 flour is flour refined to talcum powder texture. You can substitute all-purpose flour, though.

All it takes to make pasta is 00 flour and two large eggs. If you do not have a gadget, you can cut the pasta into thin strips like tagliatelle.

It is wise not to make this for the first time for a dinner party. You will not enjoy the experience if you are anxious.

INGREDIENTS

350g flour
2 large eggs

METHOD

Place the flour in the centre of a large wooden board.

Make a well. Break the eggs open and place in the centre of the well.

Beat the eggs well, and gently mix in the flour from the sides bit by bit until a dough is formed.

Knead the dough on a floured surface.

If it appears too dry or crumbly, add a little luke-warm water.

Form it into a ball, place in a bowl and cover to keep moisture in.

Roll into thin layers and put through machine or cut to desired shapes.

Place in boiling salted water and cook to your required texture.

Sauces

Apple Sauce

INGREDIENTS

500g apples, peeled, cored and sliced
3 tablespoons water
Large pinch of salt
2 teaspoons sugar
15g butter

METHOD

Place the apples and water in a saucepan and cook gently until dissolved and lumpy.

Beat to a thick purée.

Add the salt, sugar and butter, and gently reheat the sauce, stirring all the time.

Serve hot or cold.

Makes 150ml to 300ml.

Basic White Sauce

INGREDIENTS

600ml milk
30g butter
30g flour

METHOD

Melt the butter in a saucepan, add the flour and stir over a low heat for approximately 2 minutes. Add the milk.

Stir continuously over a medium heat until the sauce comes to the boil and thickens.

I sometimes add a chopped hard-boiled egg just before serving over salmon – very nutritious.

Makes approximately 600ml.

Parsley Sauce: add chopped parsley, fresh or dried.

Chocolate Sauce: add one tablespoon of cocoa when making up the basic sauce.

Custard Sauce

INGREDIENTS

2 eggs
2 teaspoons caster sugar
300ml milk
¼ teaspoon vanilla essence

METHOD

Beat the eggs and the sugar together with three tablespoons of the milk in a heat-proof bowl standing over a pan of simmering water.

Heat the rest of the milk until lukewarm and then beat in the egg mixture.

Cook without boiling until the custard thickens.

Pour into a jug and stir in the vanilla essence.

Serve hot or cold. Makes about 300ml.

Desserts and Puddings

Bread and Butter Pudding

This is a super dessert, and useful for leftover breads.

INGREDIENTS

6 thin slices of white bread, crusts removed
50g butter
40g caster sugar
50g dried fruit
600ml milk
2 eggs

METHOD

Butter the bread and cut it into small squares. Put half the squares into a buttered baking dish, and sprinkle with half the sugar and all of the fruit.

Cover with the rest of the bread, facing the buttered sides upwards.

Sprinkle with the rest of the sugar.

Beat the milk and eggs well together and pour into the dish over the bread. Leave to stand for thirty minutes.

Bake in a pre-heated moderate oven at
160°C/325°F for 45 minutes to an hour.

This dessert is super served with hot custard
and a dollop of fresh cream. I sometimes make
this a seasonal fruit pudding by adding blackber-
ries or blueberries, when in season, and grated
chocolate in winter.

Fruit Pie (Apple or Rhubarb)

INGREDIENTS

200g flour
100g butter
Pinch of salt
Water
4 medium-sized cooking apples or
8 sticks of rhubarb
Caster sugar
1 egg, beaten/milk

METHOD

Preheat oven to 180°C/350°F.

For the pastry, rub together the flour, salt and butter to breadcrumb consistency.

Make a well in the centre and carefully add water, just enough to make a dough.

Knead very little, divide in half and roll out on a floured board.

Line a greased pie dish with half of the pastry, put in your preferred filling and sprinkle with the sugar.

Cover with the remaining pastry, paint the top with beaten egg or milk and bake in the oven for 20 to 25 minutes.

Grilled Fruit Kebabs

This recipe came from my good friends Mari and Mike Hanly of Glendine B&B in Clonakilty (www.glendine.com).

INGREDIENTS

Any selection of hard fruit you like to use,
for example, 2 pears, 2 apples,
1 pineapple, 4 plums.
60g butter

METHOD

Melt the butter.

Cut the fruit into 2cm cubes.

Put the fruit on a bamboo skewer, alternating the fruit types (you must work fast to prevent the fruit turning brown).

Coat the fruit in melted butter using a pastry brush.

Sprinkle all over with caster sugar.

Place under a very hot grill for 4–5 minutes until the fruit begins to carmelise. Turn the kebabs and grill on the other side.

Serve hot with natural yogurt or ice-cream.

Ice-Cream

INGREDIENTS

280ml double cream
5 tablespoons icing sugar, sifted
2 tablespoons milk
1 teaspoon vanilla essence

METHOD

Pour the milk and cream into a chilled bowl and beat until quite thick.

Stir in the sugar and the vanilla essence, and pour into moulds or an ice cube tray. Place in the freezer* for 45 minutes.

Remove, and pour back into the chilled bowl. Break it up and stir until smooth.

Place the mixture back into the moulds or ice cube tray, and freeze for up to two hours or until solid.

Chocolate Ice-Cream: add 2 tablespoons of cocoa powder dissolved in water after the first freezing.

Chocolate Chip Ice-Cream: add 50g of grated chocolate after the first freezing.

---

* Ensure your freezer is set to the lowest temperature.

3

Strategies for Surviving in Challenging Circumstances

I list some methods of coping with the pressures of day-to-day life below, which I have used over the years and have found beneficial.

Honesty

To quote my ten-year-old daughter – 'I want to marry...sweet chilli sauce!' 'I want to marry' is a phrase she applies to any person, place or object she adores.

In fact, I want to marry honesty. I have learned that, in my life, honesty really has been, and is, the best way forward. As clichéd as this sounds, honesty really is the best policy.

There is great relief in saying to others how things really are for you. Talking about your state of mind, finances, relationships, health and career in the most candid terms not only lifts a great weight off your shoulders, but it helps other people understand the pressure you are under. Trust me! You will be shocked by just how supportive the bank manager can be once he or she knows that things aren't quite adding up because, for example, you have to pay rent for your child in college.

My own survival, to date, has been down to complete honesty with bank managers, my children, colleagues, clients, my accountant, Revenue – in fact, everyone. And, yes, occasionally a cheque has bounced and a Laser Card has been declined.

Not only does honesty help gain you understanding and allowances from those around you, but it will also help you to stay on top of everything in your life.

Concealing feelings, emotions or even secrets takes energy – precious energy that you need to address some other aspect of your day-to-day living. I'm not saying that it's easy to expose the details of your private life to those around you (and there really are some things that should be kept to yourself!). However, there are ways and means of keeping those around you tactfully informed of what is going on.

Picture this: you are at the checkout in a supermarket. You've just slid your Laser Card into the machine. It is that excruciating moment when the shop assistant is drumming her finger-tips on the counter-top and all eyes are on the Laser Card machine, awaiting authorisation. Saying something like, 'I really hope this card doesn't heave and keel over' can really lighten a tense situation and help calm your own nerves.

The truth is that lots of people have found themselves in the situation of their card being declined in this climate of recession. Checkout operators in large supermarkets expect to see the customer sweating while waiting for card authorisation, and scrutinising the receipt and questioning prices. Really, bouncing cheques and declined debit cards are nothing to be embarrassed about.

This kind of honesty can be applied to bigger situations.

In the present climate, there are in the region of 1,300 domestic disconnections per month (RTÉ News, www.rte.ie, July 2011). The past eighteen months have seen a gradual increase in the time period for paying bills. Most banks and large organisations appreciate an honest picture of your finances and will give you additional time or staggered payment options. Never ignore their letters or their warnings, because ignoring them leads to repossessions, and vital services such heating and electricity could be cut off.

When your children request luxury items, explain simply that you would provide what they want with 'all your heart' if you could, but that other more important needs have to be met first. Be assertive about it, and be prepared to repeat yourself a number of times. It may take a little time and patience, but they will eventually accept what you are saying.

Sit around the kitchen table with your children and explain the household finances to them.

Talk to them about prioritising monthly bills. Explain what a mortgage actually is. Perhaps show them a simple budget for the household. This is introducing them to a very important life skill – managing a household on a budget.

When friends approach you to go out to dinner, inform them of your situation and suggest that they come to your house instead, or that you all go out for coffee instead of a meal.

When it comes to hiring contractors or tradesmen, tell them exactly what you can afford from the outset and ask for the quote in writing. Make sure that the cost of the labour, with or without Value Added Tax (VAT), and also the cost of materials are specified clearly.

Optimism

Do you judge the glass to be half full or half empty?

Each morning, on waking, I think of all the good things in my life. I think of my daughters, my friends, my health and my pets. Following this acknowledgement of the positives in my life, I am immediately optimistic and in a better frame of mind to face the challenges ahead.

The wise person knows that the tide always turns – no life is constantly up or down. In order to be successful, we need to embrace the idea that things are not always going to be smooth sailing.

In a small example of how not dwelling on the negative can actually help buoy the economy, I noted in the summer of 2009 and in early 2010 that the German and French tourists were the customers who bought the higher priced items in my music shop. The same customers also told me that they didn't talk about or mention the recession so much in their countries. Perhaps it's a coincidence, perhaps not.

In order to think positive, I have found that spending some time each day sitting quietly and focusing on my breathing helps. This simple action will centre your energy and pull it inwards, putting you in a better place mentally to face any challenging moments throughout your day.

Look around your home. Is there any area or object that causes your energy to drop, even momentarily? Anything linked to a painful or embarrassing memory in your past needs to go – to a friend, a local charity shop, or to be recycled or sold.

Living in the 'Now'

'When?' This little word is solely responsible for all sorts of dreams and fantasies based in the 'happy ever after' future.

How many times do we delude ourselves into believing that when we achieve a material object, or marriage to Mr or Miss X, or a promotion, we will be deliriously happy, only to find that, when we do achieve those things, we are in fact not much happier at all but still in pursuit of happiness.

We can spend a lifetime pursuing objects and events based in the future and remain out of touch with the reality of the here and now. We can make huge decisions based on events or situations we imagine will happen, events that may never materialise at all.

'Does this support me?' This question can be applied to any pattern of behaviour, idea, decision or relationship in your life and, when answered honestly, can be a clear indicator of what direction to take. The question itself is based in the present tense, and in your own reality. It dispenses with 'when' and 'if'.

For example, this question applied to any relationship can clarify the issue of balance within the relationship quickly: is this person supportive of my needs?

As an experiment, try to give whatever task you are doing at any one time your 100 per cent attention. I find that this helps to control anxiety, and frightening 'what if?' and 'when?' thoughts.

I have learned to live in the now, largely due to the unexpected death of quite a few precious people in my life over the years. I think it is my most important lesson.

This is the show, not the rehearsal.

Counselling

Counselling, as I discovered in recent years, has proved to be a tremendous support to me in challenging times. We've heard the expression that counselling is 'for the mentally well'. It provides an outlet for all thoughts, emotions and anxieties in a supportive, confidential environment.

You are never alone. You can avail of counselling services through your GP, and low-cost counselling is also available (just google the key words 'low cost counselling' and a number of counselling services will appear).

Remember, there are a lot of people out there going through similar experiences. You are not the only one experiencing financial or other difficulties, though it may feel like that a lot of the time. This became obvious to me when I took part in group counselling, where members of the group spoke about the difficulties in their lives. I found I could identify with lots of the issues.

You are not wholly the role you play in your job, or the extent of your earning power or your bank balance, though you may be carrying that belief. Your true worth goes far beyond material constraints.

Grow Your Own Organic Food

We are free to choose the type of food we eat and we are faced with many options. I believe that food carries a spiritual energy within. By this, I mean the energy of the grower, factory worker, distributor, shop or supermarket staff, and anyone else involved in preparing food prior to its arrival on your table.

Eating organic food, produced without chemicals and without harm to anyone, I find gives me more clarity of mind and energy. Of course, very occasionally I have takeaway Chinese and Indian food, and I thoroughly enjoy it.

Organic fruit and vegetables tend to be more expensive than their non-organic counterparts, so it is not always realistic to buy organic.

You might look at growing your own fruit and vegetables. Polytunnels are increasing in popularity for individuals and families. These tunnels come in many sizes and they are made of galvanised steel tubing with interlocking joints covered with clear or opaque polythene. Straight or curved sides are optional. They are used to grow fruit and vegetables that need a higher temperature than the natural environment can provide. Following your initial spend on the tunnel, wheelbarrow, bamboo canes and wooden stakes, the results are worthwhile. Polytunnels range in price from €520 upwards, depending on the square footage of the tunnel. A 100 sq. ft tunnel costs in the region of €500, while a tunnel consisting of 900 sq. ft will cost you in and around €1,290. There are many sizes in between. The website www.polytunnelireland.

com lists suppliers of polytunnels in Ireland, in addition to courses, resources and books on the subject. Most suppliers will assemble the poly-tunnel, or recommend somebody reputable to assemble it.

A vegetable plot in your garden will suffice for growing a variety of vegetables if a polytunnel is beyond your means at present.

Check out www.giyireland.com for a comprehensive guide to growing your own fruit and vegetables, and other brilliant methods of self-sustainability.

Pamper Yourself

Are you minding yourself? Are you a good parent to you? Are you having three balanced meals daily and adequate sleep? For many years I was not kind to myself, nor did I acknowledge that I had needs. Now I do and I find that I am less likely to be thrown off balance from day to day.

Try to indulge in a little treat every day, for example, going on a walk, taking an aromatherapy bath, watching a comic movie, reading a funny book, having reflexology or a massage, going swimming, baking or listening to music. Seek out your local library, where there is a wealth of books and material on pampering methods.

Any activity that helps to lift your spirits in your day-to-day living is a must.

List some daily treats here:

1.
2.
3.
4.
5.

Enlist the Support of Friends and Family

According to the dictionary, to enlist means:

1. To engage a person or persons for service in the armed forces.
2. To engage the support or co-operation of a person or persons.

You need to enlist your nearest and dearest to support you in your battle to cut excess expenditure.

For this strategy to work, you need to motivate them. Following dinner, when everybody is relaxed, get each family member to write a wish list of three items they really want.

Your family's wish list might look like this:

Dad: new golf clubs, guitar, car seat covers

Teenager: new mobile phone, laptop, iPad, sports gear, clothes, make-up

Child: Nintendo 3DS, mobile phone, laptop

Mum: facial, body massage, spa treatment, theatre or cinema tickets

Each family member in turn reads one item aloud from his or her list. At this point you introduce your completed Budget Planner sheet (see Chapter 4). This should have a list of all of the projected outgoings for an average month. Read them all out.

Simply explain that, in cutting costs in as many areas as possible on this sheet, and putting by a little money regularly, each family member will have more money available to purchase the item on their wish list after a certain period of time.

Do the maths! Specify how many weeks and the amount of money saved per week it will take to purchase each item. You can use a calendar or wall chart as a visual motivation.

This works brilliantly, because each person now has an understanding of the situation as it is and feels part of a team. Turning lights off in the home when they are not necessary and other cost-cutting strategies will take on a whole new meaning for each family member, and children and teenagers will learn the important life skills of saving and budgeting for what they want.

It will also become easier for children and teenagers to accept no as an answer, and subsequently it will be easier for you to say no. In challenging circumstances, the family environment becomes more relaxed, with everybody pulling together.

4

The Household Budget and Saving on Bills

Creating the Household Budget

A budget is a financial plan detailing all your incoming monies (salary, benefits, rents, maintenance, social welfare, etc.) and outgoing monies (mortgage, rent, food, utility bills, loan repayments, etc.).

Governments have budgets, as do large corporate organisations, educational institutions, companies in the retail sector, etc. Every successful enterprise budgets and reviews the budget regularly.

Budgeting helps you to make an assessment of your current financial situation and to plan for future expenditure. If you are in financial difficulty and involved in a legal process with financial institutions and solicitors, a household budget can act as a shield and save legal costs. When these organisations realise what your situation actually is, they may stop pursuing you or they may at least alleviate the pressure they are putting on you.

Before drawing up a budget, it is a good idea to get a clear picture of your household expenditure. Keep every receipt for every purchase in a drawer for a complete month. Carry with you some small Post-its and, where the purchase is too small to warrant a receipt, record it on a Post-it and add it to the receipts. The iPhone has quite a few 'aids to shopping' applications, useful for storing your set shopping list and prices. Some of these applications alert you daily to bargains in certain stores, but most of these are US based. I look forward to the development of applications relevant to stores in Ireland and the UK.

At the end of the month, divide the receipts into categories. For example:

- Food and groceries
- CDs/DVDs
- Alcohol and cigarettes
- Books and magazines
- Entertainment/eating out/haircuts
- Medical
- Public transport (train, bus, taxi)
- Car (petrol, insurance and tax)
- Mortgage or rent
- Electricity, heating oil and house insurance
- After-school activities

Think about which expenses you could change or reduce and which have to remain constant. What can you do without? Perhaps list these things here:

1.
2.
3.
4.
5.

On the budget planning sheet below, list all monies coming into the household in the INCOM-INGS column and all expenses in the OUTGOINGS column.

Current Monthly Budget Planning Sheet

Outgoings	€	Incomings	€
Rent or mortgage		My salary/pension	
Mortgage insurance		Partner's salary/	
House insurance		pension	
Medical insurance/		My social welfare	
expenses		Partner's social	
Food and groceries		welfare	
Electricity bills		Child Benefit	
Heating oil/gas bills		Maintenance	
TV licence		Rent	
Telephone landline		Education Allowance	
Mobile phone		Education Grant	
Internet		Other	
Cable TV			
Life insurance			
Petrol/diesel			
Travel to work cost			
Travel to school cost			
Car loan			
Car tax			
Car insurance			
Parking/tolls			
Childcare			
Household charge			
TOTAL		**TOTAL**	

Once you have completed your budget planner, subtract your total outgoings from your incomings.

At this point, there are three possible results:

1. The amount of your incomings exceeds your outgoings.

2. Both amounts are equal, so you are just managing.
3. Your outgoings exceed your incomings and you are in debt.

Whatever your result, try to keep a positive mindset. There are areas in which you can cut costs.

You should now have a good idea of what you can save per month towards debt repayments and/or holidays, birthdays, Christmas, college education, your retirement, etc.

Arrange your debts and/or items to put money aside for in order of priority, and schedule due payment dates daily, weekly, and monthly.

If you find you are in debt or you're sailing close to the wind in terms of getting into debt, it is a good idea to look at how you can cut household costs and perhaps at ways in which you can increase your income.

Saving Money on Household Bills

How to Save on Electricity Bills

Beware of signing contracts with so called 'cheaper' electricity suppliers. Very often they are not cheaper as there are often unexpected charges, such as nasty €500 penalties if you break the contract or leave the Direct Debit payment structure. These charges are always on the contract, albeit in tiny print, and are not obvious on the page where you actually sign. I got sucked into signing one of these contracts. Read any contract three times before signing.

Switch from regular light bulbs to economy bulbs. Where you have six to eight recessed lights in the ceiling, use a table lamp instead, when bright lighting is not required. Why light eight bulbs when you can light one? Install dimmer switches. Where you need low lighting, like in a TV room, why not light an aromatherapy candle rather than a lamp?

Install an electric instant shower, which is brilliant economically because you are only heating the amount of water you need. For a range of water-saving products go to www.renergise.ie.

Try not to heat your water in your immersion heater with the electric switch. Instead, have hot water as a by-product of heating your house, through gas/oil heating or solar panels.

Look at investing in solar panels. This power source, which turns the sun's energy into electricity, works all year round, even in winter. The system can be installed in a matter of days, normally on a south-facing roof, freestanding in your garden or attached to a wall. The cost depends on the size of the system. With solar panels, you can save up to 30 per cent annually on your heating bills.

Solar shingles are an alternative to panels, if you require solar power without looking like you have solar power. They were first released in 2005 and are designed to look like asphalt shingles. There are a few different types available and they are sometimes referred to as building integrated photovoltaics (BIPV). A thinner shingle will be available in the near future. These shingles produce between 13 and 63 watts. Approximately 77 tiles will cover 100 sq. ft of roof. Some shingles available are constructed of silicon – the material used in solar panels.

There are government grants available to households to help fund solar panels and other energy-saving methods. You can avail of a grant of up to €800 through the Better Energy programme, though you must undertake a Building Energy Rating (BER) assessment after any grant-aided work has been completed. It is now, by law, necessary to have this done on all properties on the open market. Your property is more saleable if it has a good rating.

Other grants available include:

- Attic insulation (€200)
- Wall insulation – cavity (€320)
- Wall insulation – external (€4,000)
- Wall insulation – internal dry lining (€2,000)
- High efficiency oil/gas boiler with controls upgrade (€560)
- Heating controls upgrade only (€400)

Check out the Sustainable Energy Authority Ireland website (www.seai.ie) for a complete picture.

More tips for saving on electricity:

- Switch appliances off completely; do not leave them on standby.
- Try to pay your bill by standing order, the same amount monthly. Ask the company how much you paid for electricity in total over the previous twelve months. Then divide this figure by twelve to get your monthly standing order amount. This way you can keep a closer check and you are less likely to get a nasty surprise in the form of a monstrous bill. Pay for your heating oil in the same way.
- Run dishwashers and washing machines only when full. Set your fridge temperature to 4°C, and your freezer to –18°C. Energy is wasted at temperatures below these.
- How dirty are your clothes? Probably not very much generally; they may just need freshening. Most washing machines have a 30°C to 40°C short cycle, lasting from twenty to thirty minutes. Use this cycle rather than a longer one.
- Try not to tumble dry your clothes. Hang them outside to dry as much as possible, or set up a washing line in your garage or porch.
- Look at your electricity metre daily, take a reading and work out how many units you are actually using. Check bills to find out whether they are estimated and way over what they should be. Submit your own reading to the electricity company regularly.

- Heat just the rooms you are using. Check that your loft insulation is sufficient. Turn your thermostat down, or the individual thermostats on radiators. You can reduce your fuel use by 10 per cent by turning down your radiators by just 1 degree.

I am including my most recent electric bill on the next page – the lowest to date at time of writing!

How to Save on Waste Bills

You can save up to 50 per cent on waste disposal costs. Recycling is the cheapest, as well as being the most environmentally friendly, option. It costs just €3 to go into my local recycling centre. Any recyclable items are free to dispose of, while standard black bags cost €4 per bag.

I spend between €15 and €20 monthly on waste disposal (approximately €240 annually). Before I recycled, the cost was €440 per year.

I was surprised at the range of items that are recyclable:

- Cardboard
- Newspapers and magazines
- Glass bottles and jars
- Plastic bottles
- Flat glass
- Scrap metal
- Paint

- Electrical items
- Beverage and food cans
- Engine oil; cooking oil
- Batteries
- Green waste
- Textiles
- DIY waste
- Timber

Remember, you can recycle all the above without charge, save for your entry fee to the recycling centre.

These amenity sites also accept many other items, with a set charge for each. It is not always necessary to hire a skip. Larger items like mattresses cost €10–€20, sofas cost €20, carpets cost €15 and a single armchair costs €10 to dispose of. You may find a local 'man with a van' to transport these to the site for a small charge, a fraction of the cost of skip hire. Alternatively, you could use Free Ads or www.donedeal.ie to sell these items for anything you can get.

Shopping – Money-Saving Tips

I covered money-saving tips for buying food in Chapter 1. Here, I outline some tips for shopping in general, for yourself and your children, and also any pets.

First, buying takeaway coffee when out and about is costly – limit yourself to drinking it out once a week as a treat.

When shopping for clothes, stick to classic cuts that will last. Before you purchase at all, ask yourself if the garment is absolutely necessary or if you can do without it. Remove temptation by avoiding boutiques and the clothes areas of large stores.

If you are in real need of an outfit for a special occasion, for instance a wedding, think about hiring one. If this is not an option, only venture out when you have established a price limit in your mind.

When you are limited to a tight budget, you are forced to purchase the most economical brand. But, should your circumstances allow at any point, try to support the Irish economy and buy Irish produced clothes. Check out www.madein irelandproject.com for a list of Irish designers.

Watch out for impulse buys – shops often strategically place items next to the cash register so that, when you are paying, you will be tempted by these items that you had not planned to buy and you do not need.

Shopping for Babies and Children

Whether to breastfeed or not is a decision made for many reasons, I know, but I found breastfeeding my babies for as long as possible helped me reduce my costs, since it cut out formula milk and sterilising bottles. It also lightens the load you have to carry around with your baby. By the time I got to baby three (I was totally laid back about it all at this stage!), I had dispensed with the extra luggage by simply carrying with me in my hand-bag two emergency nappies, a tiny pack of wipes and a very small jar of Sudocrem.

I also noted that baby rice tasted very like semo-lina (I wasn't eating it – honestly!) so I substituted it with semolina and cooked pears and apples, which I puréed myself. For drinks, I diluted fruit juice with cooled boiled water, four to one.

This was a big saving, and by the time Baby was on solids her food was whatever was on the dinner table, albeit blended – chicken, beef or lamb, and vegetables. Vanilla ice-cream proved a massive hit, and was a reward for finishing the main course.

It was the year 2000 when I had my last baby, and I was living in the UK. I was very interested to note a trend in the UK towards mums using reus-able cloth nappies. Nowadays, in Ireland, cloth nappies are readily available and are growing in popularity daily in this climate of recession. Go to www.littlecomfort.com for a super range from an Irish company. At time of writing, the company lists a complete set for €243.10. This will save you an absolute fortune on disposables.

However, a word of caution – there is an increased risk of infection with cloth nappies. Tread carefully and exercise scrupulous hygiene. If you do not want to use cloth nappies all of the time, then maybe use disposable nappies half of the time, which would still lead to some savings. Perhaps keep the disposables for night-time usage.

Do shop in charity shops for clothing for your babies and children. Remember, your children are growing quickly and all clothes are destined to be recycled after a relatively short period of time. Very often, children's clothes that end up in charity shops have never been worn. So why not do a good deed, support a charity shop and clothe your babies for less money? Toys and books are also plentiful in these shops. Generally, it helps to buy children's clothes a size or two larger. From about age five, children can be a little more conscious of their appearance, so you may need to take account of this.

Where footwear is concerned, always have the child's feet measured professionally and ensure that the shoes fit. There are huge postural and developmental implications from badly fitting shoes.

Children's birthday parties can be costly, especially when a lot of your child's friends have their birthdays around the same time of year. A brilliant idea I heard about recently was that each child put €5 in a card for the child whose birthday it was. This was on the initiative of the birthday child's parents. Lots of parents were relieved with this, and it really is a very low-cost, practical answer to a potentially expensive and sometimes unexpected event.

Make birthday cards at home – this can be a lot of fun for your child. Introduce your child to clip art on the computer. Children get hours of fun from this activity and then they can email their cards to friends and relatives. Children as young as four years (under supervision) can do this.

Another alternative for children and adults is to send an e-card. For the price of two or three traditional paper cards you can subscribe to www.jacquielawson.com and send an unlimited number of e-cards in a year. These are very beautiful. I received one called 'The Olive Tree' from a friend and I love it.

Schoolbooks are now mostly available second hand, and some schools run a book rental scheme where you pay only a fraction of the book costs and return the books at the end of the school year.

Some bookshops offer a 'trade-in' service, which means that they accept the old school books in part payment against the new. This can also be done online – it involves emailing the shop a list of your own books and your required new ones, and they will quickly and efficiently offer you a price in part exchange. The website www.schoolbookexchange. ie is a free service, and you can purchase and sell second-hand books for school and college here with an average saving of 66 per cent.

Shopping for Teenagers

Mobile phones are a huge part of the teen social networking system, and are also important for their safety and sense of security. Shop around the major networks for the best-value mobile phones and tariffs, and ask them about the most economical package for teens currently on offer. Never stay loyal to any particular network because the best package moves from network to network as they jostle for the biggest portion of the market.

Some teens are designer-label conscious, both boys and girls, and this really can be a nightmare in terms of the emotional and financial pressure they can put on you to provide them with designer clothes and goods. Since the recession began, my teenagers have been researching the market for cheaper designer labels. They succeeded! They found TK Maxx, the discount store for labels, and they hunted on the internet and found quite a few American websites selling Roxy, Abercrombie and other labels for less money. I found websites offering clothes at $5.99 or less for each item.

Check out the following websites, listed as 'the hottest teen stores online': www.599fashion.com, www.theoutlet.com and www.tkmaxx.com.

American Eagle, Alloy, Charlotte Russe, Forever 21, Fred Flare, Urban Outfitters and Wet Seal all have offers on their websites and they deliver to Ireland.

However, if you can persuade your teenager that if it looks good on you, it really doesn't matter whether it is a designer garment or not, you've really hit the jackpot.

Do exercise care when shopping online, and use PayPal or a prepaid credit card.

Shopping for Pets

Tinned foods, especially brand names and dried foods, though succulent for our furry friends, prove expensive. You can make this go further by boiling pasta or rice and adding it to the tinned dog or cat food.

My dogs and cats are fed leftovers from our table when they are available – pasta, vegetables, meat, soup, bread, stocks and gravies. This food is always welcomed and devoured. I never feed them chicken or chop bones, as these are sharp and can fragment easily, causing the animal to choke. I very often cook a pot of rice with butcher's bones and leftover bread for the animals.

In the supermarkets, late in the day and early in the morning, there is very often bread on special offer or at a reduced price, especially rolls and batons, left over from the previous day. These are useful fillers.

Be Aware of Benefits

If you have recently become unemployed, or are divorced, widowed or homeless – or, in fact, none of these – there is a lot of help and support available to you from Government.

You may be missing out on tax reliefs. Go to Revenue's website (www.revenue.ie) to see what tax relief may be applicable to you.

I urge you to look into the benefits that might apply to you. You may be pleasantly surprised. Go to your local social welfare office, introduce yourself with your personal public service (PPS) number and they will put you in the picture fairly quickly regarding the financial support available to you.

Below is a list of possible benefits, some of which may apply to your situation. Please note that this is not an exhaustive list.

Benefits available in Ireland:

- Supplementary Welfare Allowance
- Rent and Mortgage Interest Supplement
- Special Needs Supplement
- Exceptional Needs Supplement
- Urgent Needs Payment
- Back to School Clothing and Footwear Allowance
- Family Income Supplement
- Farm Assist
- Jobseeker's Allowance
- Back to Education Allowance

- Back to Work Enterprise Allowance
- Part-Time Job Incentive Scheme
- Employers' PRSI Exemption Scheme
- Revenue Job Assist
- Treatment Benefit
- Bereavement Grant
- National Fuel Scheme
- Smokeless Fuel Allowance
- Free Travel
- Household Benefits Package
- Living Alone Increase
- Increase for Living on a Specified Island
- Rent Allowance (for tenants affected by the de-control of rents)
- Illness Benefit
- Invalidity Pension
- Disability Allowance
- Blind Pension
- Carer's Benefit
- Carer's Allowance
- Respite Care Grant
- Injury Benefit
- Disablement Benefit
- Medical Care
- Death Benefits – Widow or Widower's Pension, Funeral Grant
- Jobseeker's Benefit
- Child Benefit
- Maternity Benefit
- Adoptive Benefit
- Health and Safety Benefit

- Guardian's Payment (Contributory and Non-Contributory)
- School Meals Programme
- One Parent Family Benefit
- Widowed Parent Grant
- Widow or Widower's Contributory Pension
- Widow or Widower's Non-Contributory Pension

Ways of Generating Extra Income

Most people are working harder now, for less wages. They are also diversifying in the services and products they are offering.

For example, when a man was selling garden utensils before, he may now be offering garden furniture as well, and a grass-cutting service. Teachers who were giving grinds in one subject might now be offering grinds in two or three subjects.

What can you do? Begin by writing down your skills and strong points below:

1.
2.
3.
4.
5.

Now list any possibilities or opportunities you may have for using these skills to make extra money:

1.
2.
3.
4.
5.

Consider these questions and ideas:

* What are you really well informed about? What skills have you got that you are not using?
* What do people need that you might be able to offer?
* Have you got old furniture or antiques lying about, or anything that you might sell in a garage sale or car boot sale?
* Could you do part-time jobs, for example, house sitting; pet sitting or pet exercising; light gardening; babysitting; giving music, art, crochet or knitting classes; grinds; ironing and housework – and so on.
* Can you make or grow things to sell?
* How about inventing a gadget to make house-work easier (think of James Dyson, the inventor of the 'bag-less' vacuum cleaner – genius!).
* Are you good at selling? Could you sell someone else's product(s)?
* Take a course in reflexology or something similar and offer it as a service.

There are many courses now available free of charge for people to upskill. Check out the springboard incentive on www.bluebrick.ie and www. springboard.ie.

5

Hiring Contractors for Work
around the House

An increasing number of homeowners are finding themselves in negative equity as the market value of their home falls below the outstanding mortgage debt owed to the financial institution.

It makes solid financial sense not to sell your property at the moment when prices are low, unless you really have to. Since people may not be as free to move house as before, home improvements may be the answer to any problems. Loft conversions, extensions and solar panels are also a means towards increasing the market value of your home.

I began to renovate properties in 1997, following the ending of a relationship. A friend, realising I was rather down, suggested that I improve my then dreary dilapidated house. He suggested that I use some of my savings.

I responded with, 'I am keeping those for a rainy day.'

He looked at me, smiled and said, 'Don't you think it is raining in your life now?'

It was – it was positively torrential.

So, with stubborn determination, I set about transforming my environment.

That was the beginning of my journey through the maze of home renovation, which was sometimes smooth, other times stormy. Things did not always go to plan, but I learned so much in the process. I learned what jobs I could manage around the house and what jobs I could not. I learned the hard way. At times my mistakes proved expensive and caused me a great deal of stress.

I have renovated three houses, two in the UK and one in Ireland, and I feel confident in hiring tradesmen.

Presently there is a general optimistic belief that a 'Debt Forgiveness Bill' will be passed in the near future, allowing people to repay what they can afford on their mortgages, based on their means. Unfortunately, there is no guarantee that this will come about.

Steps to Hiring the Best Contractor for the Job

First, establish what work around the house you can manage yourself. Electrical, plumbing and carpentry work needs to be done by qualified, insured tradespeople.

I could tell you some pretty hair-raising stories about builders, and I am sure you may know some yourself. But there are also some stories of excellence. Here are a few tips for hiring a contractor:

- Before hiring anybody, get recommendations from friends and neighbours. This will quickly give you a shortlist. Do not start with the phone directory – anybody, qualified or not, can place an advertisement in the yellow pages.
- Check for the contractor's insurance and their work record; request at least three references. Ask lots and lots of questions, pen in hand, and jot down the answers. Do not be afraid to demand to see their insurance certification. You are at risk if the tradesperson is without insurance.
- Find out if they are involved in any legal dispute, or if there is any complaint against them.
- Arrange an appointment to meet them and look at some of their previous work. You should try to meet at least three contractors.
- Get a quote from each contractor *in writing*, clearly outlining costs of materials, labour and VAT, and the expected duration of the work. Every tiny detail needs to be accounted for in the quote. Should things go horribly wrong, verbal agreements are worthless in court. There are jobs that the contractor actually has to start before they can see the full extent of the work. In this

case, ask for a figure that the overall cost will not exceed so that there is a definite cap. Never agree to pay by the hour. This means that you are going to be anxiously looking at your watch on the hour, every hour, doing the math in your head. It also means that your tradesperson can go at a snail's pace on a whim. Insist on a price for the entire job and prepare to be assertive.

- If you can't get a straight reply on the issue of cost or if there is any reluctance to provide references, move on to the next applicant.
- Be consistent about your requests from contractor to contractor. Check out the attitude of each contractor. Remember that this person in going to be in and around your home. If you have any uneasy feeling at all, and if they seem in any way reluctant, impatient or brusque, just move on to the next one. When you have quotes from three different contractors, compare the materials (type and cost), the cost of labour and the expected duration of the work. Where there are big differences between the quotes, ask why.
- Beware of the quote that seems incredibly cheap – more than likely this is not a good prospect, because the materials may be of low quality and/or the workers under qualified.
- Never pay up front. Stage payments are a good idea, if it is a large undertaking like a new build or an extension. Do get your solicitor involved to vet the contract and oversee it. Most reputable builders have separate accounts for building

materials with suppliers, so requests for money for materials up front are not necessary.
- For smaller jobs, pay the tradesman when the job has been completed to your satisfaction.

Be attentive while the work is going on. If the colour of the paint is incorrect, or the bath or radiator is in the wrong position, shout. It's a bit late to tell the contractor when the work is finished.

I made this mistake during a renovation. The workers were replacing first floor joists, and I had left them with the materials. I had discussed the job with their boss in detail, pointing out where the window was so that they would allow for it. He went off to another job and I went to work.

On returning that night, I went to look at the work that had been done that day. To my horror, I noticed that they had not allowed for the window. Three joists were in the wrong position, and, worse still, were set in concrete.

Next morning, first thing, I went to meet them – two huge burly types (no sign of the boss). I assertively stated that there was a problem and that the joists would have to be redone. They tried to bypass the problem to avoid pulling the joists back out and redoing them. I remained stubborn and insisted.

In the end, they did what I asked. That proved a very tense and anxious time for me, and, I have no doubt, was also difficult for them.

Keep a diary and/or photographic record each day of what work is completed (and what is not!). My children had great fun recording one extension from foundation to completion. The builders didn't mind.

Treat contractors kindly and they will do a better job. You may find yourself in a position where you have to fire the contractor. This is never pleasant, but if the work is bad it is going to cost you a lot of money to have it undone and then redone.

Once you have signed a contract, you must continue to pay someone, unless the work is not proceeding as in your contract, or there is drug or alcohol abuse, aggressive confrontational behaviour, theft, damage to personal property, bad quality workmanship, or inconsistency in attending the site. Consult your solicitor and photograph the site or parts of it prior to dismissing the contractor. It is always a good idea to talk to an expert before you take action, to check your own perception of the situation.

For eco-friendly and economical building methods and sustainable living, check out http://theholliesonline.com.

6

Buying a Car

How do you choose which car to buy? What make and model? New or second hand?

First, what can you really afford? For the car type of your choice, look at the actual running costs and the mandatory insurance and road tax, combined with the daily costs of petrol/diesel, servicing and tyres.

In a nutshell, the bigger the engine capacity of the car, the more expensive it will be to run. Purchase the smallest car you can that will meet your needs. Be practical in your choice. Have you got a growing family, pets and a double bass to transport? You must choose the size of your car accordingly. When recruiting young players for double bass lessons in the UK, I had to inform the parents that it might mean a change of car to an estate, to warn them in advance so they would not be suddenly pressured financially if their offspring proved to be a prodigy on the instrument.

When faced with the choice of three or five doors, five is best for ease of moving babies, transporting grandparents, shopping, and lifting anything in and out of the back seat.

New or Used?

New and used cars depreciate in value as time elapses. Some models have a higher depreciation value than others. A car is an investment, so you want the best possible value for your money. Bearing this in mind, a more expensive car is not necessarily a better investment than a cheaper car with slower depreciation.

By the time an average car reaches one year old, it has lost approximately 40 per cent of its initial value. The website www.whatcar.com has a depreciation index calculator that allows you to compare the depreciation of up to four cars. Examples of family cars that hold value better than other makes are the Nissan Qashqai 1.6 Visia, the Volkswagen Golf and the Honda Civic.

By the time your car reaches three years old, it has lost 60 per cent of its value, allowing for an average mileage of 12,000km to 15,000km per year. If you do more mileage than the average, it depreciates even more.

Keeping this in mind, it is perhaps the best way forward to buy an almost-new car, as the next best thing to new and much cheaper, or a four- or five-year-old car, because it has already lost most of its value by then. Purchase from a reputable car dealer because if anything goes wrong, they will rectify the problem.

Before Purchasing

Having decided the size of car to suit your needs, the model and, if you are buying second hand, the year, it is time to start researching and looking in earnest.

Look in as many garages as you can, and keep a log of all cars of the same type, mileage, colour and year. Look in newspapers and car magazines, comparing like with like. Be prepared to do the groundwork for at least two months.

You are looking for the car with the least mileage relative to year, and in good condition inside and out. After a while, you will be able to spot the better purchases, with lower mileage and price. Eventually one or two cars will stand out for you as being the best possibilities.

Now comes the fun bit! You have to do a little bit of haggling for your car. Never offer the asking price. Express an interest, test drive it and check that switches work. Survey the body for scratches and indentations, and check tyres and wipers for wear.

If anything needs doing, make a note of it – it may come in useful in the bargaining process.

Make an opening offer of at least a €1,000 to €1,200 less than the asking price, and be prepared to walk away, leaving your contact number. Tell the salesperson that this is one of two cars you are interested in. You will have to subtly assess the salesperson here, to decide how tough a nut they are. Remember, they really want to sell this car to you.

Be stubborn – you are looking to reach a sale price somewhere in the middle of what you are offering to pay and what they are asking, along with agreement from them to do the small jobs that need doing, such as fitting new tyres, brakes or windscreen wipers. Asking for the car to be serviced by the garage is a good last-minute request before clinching the deal.

Keep this in your mind – if you don't manage to secure this deal, there will be others. Try not to become too attached to one particular car.

Just before you hand over your cash, go onto www.motorcheck.ie, put in the car registration, and for €120 you will get a full history of the car and whether it has been crashed or has been off the road for a time.

You can also pay for an AA Car Data Check, where the car is inspected by an expert and anything that is in poor working order or is unsafe will be highlighted to you.

Paying for these checks is a way of ensuring your own peace of mind. For a tiny fraction of the price of your intended purchase, you are guaranteeing a good investment for your hard-earned money.

If both of these checks yield positive results, go ahead with your purchase.

Choosing Finance Options

There are quite a few finance options available. You can go through your bank or lending institution by getting a personal loan and repaying it over a set period of time.

Hire purchase (HP) is another option. This means the company owns the car until you pay it off in full. You need a deposit of 10 to 15 per cent of the price, or a car to trade as part payment. Selling the car you have bought on HP is not an option until you have fully paid for it. One variation on this is termed a 'balloon payment'. This means that a large part of the loan is left to be paid off at the end of the agreement. This makes the monthly payments lower.

You can also lease the car. This means that you agree with the leasing company a set period of time for which you will have the car and a set mileage that you will use. Payments are fixed following an initial deposit. At the end of the agreed period, you may wish to give the car back without owing anything. If you do go over the agreed mileage, the leasing company can charge you extra. Should you decide to own the car, you will need to pay a lump sum termed 'the guaranteed future value'. The advantage of leasing is that all servicing, maintenance and repair are done by the leasing company. I leased a small Opel Corsa in the 1990s and, at the outset, the agreed mileage seemed more than adequate, but I still managed to exceed it and I had to pay £900 when returning the car. If you do choose to go this route, try to overestimate your mileage and weigh up the resulting effect on the monthly payments.

The dealer's finance package does not always guarantee the best deal. Shop around. If you have a loan arranged before you go into the car show-room, you are a cash buyer and therefore are in a stronger bargaining position. Also, if it is an unse-cured loan, you can sell your car at any time, but you will still need to repay the loan. Compare the final amount you will have paid back in total by the time you reach the end of the payments to spot the best deal between corporate lenders.

If you pay off the loan earlier than the agreed duration, penalty early repayment fees apply. You will pay the balance in addition to an agreed penalty based on a percentage of the projected interest repayable over the duration of the contract. Read the small print.

You need to consider payment protection insur-ance, to cover you if you should fall ill or if you have an accident and are unable to make loan repayments. This can be a monthly or a once-off payment – shop around for the cheapest, and read the fine print extremely carefully. There may be exclusions, or payments may not begin until three months following the event.

Some General Tips for Buying
Used Cars Privately

- It is very difficult to judge the safety of your investment on first appearance.
- The mileage may be tampered with, even the digital displays. In some cases you may be looking at two cars expertly welded together, previously two write-offs masquerading as one sound vehicle. Do an AA Car Check to be sure.
- The appearance of the pedals, steering wheel and dashboard should tie in with the mileage on the clock. Well-worn pedals and a shiny steering wheel indicate a lot of miles. Also, ensure you see the National Car Testing (NCT) history and the registration papers of the car.
- Be prepared to contact previous owners about the mileage and history. As a previous owner, I was contacted only once, by the buyer of an Opel Astra that I had for a time, two years following the sale.
- Very occasionally, the number plate may be stolen from another car of the same make, model, year and colour. Plates are easily made and fitted to a stolen car. This is called cloning. Do an AA Check, for total peace of mind.
- See the car, with a friend for your security, at a registered address in daylight, never in a car park or at the roadside.
- Check the car's service history – mileage will be recorded at each service.

- Be wary of seeming bargains – they seldom are bargains at all.
- Test drive the car.
- If you are even slightly uneasy, or have any doubts at all, leave it. There are lots of other cars out there.
- Never hand over money until you have the keys, the paperwork and the car, and the seller has signed the forms.

Internet Car Shopping

This is the most risky way of purchasing a car. It is very easy to be duped here. By all means, do use the internet to compare prices in relation to similar makes/models and mileage. I used this to my advantage when purchasing a car for my daughter, but in the end I bought from a reputable dealer, with my homework done, and a good idea of the particular model and price in my mind.

The first questions to ask would be whether you know the firm you are buying the car from, and whether the firm actually exists or is a cyber fairytale.

If you do decide to press the BUY button, print off all the dealer's details, and the description of the car, the quote and, most importantly, the completed order form.

There has been an increase in scams on the internet, where people have paid out money expecting a car to be delivered and it never arrived. In fact, there has been such an increase in fraud in the UK that the bigger sellers – ebay, Auto Trader, and Exchange and Mart – have joined forces with the police in an effort to combat crime. They have formed the Vehicle Safe Trading Advisory Group (www.vstag.co.uk).

Consumer Rights

In general, the car you purchase needs to meet all aspects of the sale description. If the description specified heated seats, an immobiliser and CD changers then it must be 100 per cent true. Everything must be in working order.

The car must be of a standard or quality that a 'reasonable person' would deem acceptable.

After weeks, even months, if the car does not live up to the quality you were led to expect, you are within your rights to go back to the dealer with it.

However, if they recommended you have the car thoroughly checked before you purchased it, and you didn't do this, then you do not have any legal rights.

Purchasing from a private seller is a riskier way forward, because they are under no legal obligation to provide any aftercare of satisfactory quality.

How to Cut Down on the Running Costs of Your Car

- Your fuel costs will be lessened if you drive as smoothly as possible, changing gears when appropriate to avoid the engine labouring. Drive at a steady pace – heavy acceleration equals heavy fuel consumption. Service your car regularly to ensure that your engine is functioning efficiently using the least amount of fuel.
- Tyre pressure needs to be correct – check it frequently and maintain it according to your car manual. Underinflated tyres are prone to overheating and suffer more damage, while over-inflating your tyres leads to poor car handling. You achieve optimum fuel efficiency with correct levels and this helps the environment with lower CO_2 emissions.
- Use air conditioning sparingly.
- Compare fuel prices in the petrol stations close by and fill up where it is cheapest.
- Before starting a journey to any destination, try to plan and fit in as many other jobs as possible on the way, so as to achieve maximum benefit from one trip. People are now much more conscious of fuel consumption since the price of fuel rocketed early this year. How necessary is the journey? Can you car pool or lift share?
- Remember, small cars are the most economical choice, as all associated costs are cheaper.

7

Insurance – How to Get the Best Deal

Researching Quotations

My friend Vera, who has been on this planet forty years longer than I have, and has a lot more experience with shopping for cheap car and house insurance, says: 'Get at least six quotes.' Have pen and paper in hand, and be prepared to spend between two to three hours researching quotations. Keep in mind that it will be worthwhile in the end. As you list the companies and quotes, you will see quite a diversity in costs, excesses and extras. You can call these companies yourself and/or browse the internet. My teenager was delegated this task on lots of occasions. After a few hours, she presented me with the cheapest quote and the number to call.

For car and house insurance, try to get a handle on the current worth of your car and house (including contents) before you call any insurance providers for quotations. Make sure you are insuring for the correct value and not over-insuring. Never accept the first quote you receive from each company. Carefully clarify the excess payment in your verbal query and make a note of this (the excess is the amount of the damage you will pay for yourself, in the event of a claim, before your insurer pays the balance). Look at the proposal form and accompanying documentation when it reaches you to check whether the quote and, indeed, everything else is the same as what was given to you verbally, and that you under-stand everything in the documentation.

Read All Documentation

Be wary of the accompanying booklet that arrives with the proposal form. This contains all sorts of conditions and exclusions.

Read this booklet in the bath, on the loo, in any spare moments you can find. You may be surprised at the contents. Things you might have thought would be insured are possibly not.

Unfortunately, I have fallen victim on the house insurance front. A number of years ago, I had to rent out a property to make ends meet. I went through a reputable letting agent and agreed to let it to a family. Brilliant references were provided by the tenants to the agent (I found out subsequently that these were all false), but, after repairing quite a few appliances, I decided to call an end to the agreement six months later.

When I saw the state of the house on repossession, I was horrified. There was €16,000 to €17,000 worth of damage done, which was not obvious on first sight. I was advised that if I pursued the tenant through the courts, I might be waiting years for full compensation. So I contacted my insurance company through my broker. What followed was a long road that led to disappointment.

First, I was told I had to pay an excess payment of €3,000. This had not appeared on the proposal form I signed to take out the policy, but details were in the accompanying booklet, which I did not have time to read before signing the proposal.

At that point, I panicked. I did not have €3,000 to fund any part of the claim. I couldn't tell if the damage was just cosmetic (broken glass, filth, broken solid oak kitchen doors) or more serious, like central heating, electrics, or worse, so I alerted the insurance company to a pending claim and went to the property to start the clear-up.

I realise now that the correct way forward would have been to hire an independent insurance assessor, send them in to assess the scene and let them handle the entire claim for a small percentage of the claim settlement. But this was my first-ever claim on my house insurance in twenty-six years of diligently and obediently paying premiums on time.

This is what followed. The insurance company contacted me and asked me if I wanted to let their assessor handle it or get my own. Not knowing very much and wishing to proceed as quickly as possible, I agreed to their assessor. Very big mistake!

After an initial five weeks, they offered me less than a third of the monies claimed. When I refused to accept this, they came back four to six weeks later with another, slightly higher offer. I finally got less than a third – €7,800 of the cost of the total damages including the excess of €3,000 (so what I actually got was €4,800). Had I continued haggling for weeks on end, I'm sure I might have gotten more. But I was struggling financially and I had no choice. I am including this story in the hope that it will urge people to acquire their own assessors for any insurance claim (and, ultimately, to read the documentation!).

Always insure new for old. This totally rules out whether any damage claimed for can be deemed 'normal wear and tear' by the insurance company. In insuring new for old, the insurance company must replace the item or provide the full cost of the item newly purchased in the event of any damage. In my own claim for damages, my property and house contents prior to the let were new. The insurance company claimed that the damage to floors (burns and deep scratches) and walls was normal wear and tear and the damage was not paid for.

Car Insurance

When insuring your car, do you really need comprehensive insurance or will third party fire and theft insurance cover you? The difference between these two options is as follows:

- Third party fire and theft cover should pay for any damage you do to someone else's vehicle, and will cover damage to your car in the event of it catching fire, being stolen or being the object of attempted theft.
- Comprehensive insurance covers all of the above and all damage to your own car, whether you or someone else is to blame.

The former is normally the cheaper option. Thankfully, when I had to claim from car insurance companies in the past, I was reimbursed for all damage efficiently.

Reviewing Value

In Dublin in 2007 the property bubble burst, and, by the opening months of 2010, property had decreased in value rapidly. In south Dublin, three-bedroom duplexes that previously sold at around €770,000 eventually sold for €300,000. The general accepted average figure by which the value of property has fallen on a national scale is around 40 per cent. In this context, it is worth reviewing your current insurance to check the actual value of your property against the premium, even if you have remained loyal to one insurer for quite a good many years.

Remember that your car is decreasing in value from year to year also, and the amount you insured it for initially is not what it is worth now. Quite a lot of the time, when the renewal comes through the post, we do not have the time or patience to deal with it, so we tend to sign it and return it without a thought. This is an area where you can make substantial savings, just by taking a little more time with it.

8

Twelve Ways to Cut Legal Costs

Buying and selling property (conveyancing), making a will, separating or divorcing, signing leases (corporate and domestic), or affidavits (witnessed sworn statements of fact or facts) are circumstances for which you are likely to have need for a solicitor.

Where the legal profession is concerned, there is not a standard price list to peruse. All cases are individual. But there are some standard costs, should you need a solicitor or a barrister to represent you in court or while in police custody.

Time really is money when these legal eagles preside in their offices, and they charge approximately €250 per hour (€4.16 per minute). Whatever your circumstances, the following twelve pointers will help you cut your legal costs substantially.

1. Shop Around

Email or fax your requirements to at least four solicitors and obtain a written quotation from each one. Section 68 of the Solicitors (Amendment) Act 1994 states that:

> 'On the taking of instructions to provide legal services to a client, or as soon as is practicable thereafter, a solicitor shall provide the client with particulars in writing of
>
> a. The actual charges or
>
> b. Where the provision of the actual charge or an estimate of such charges is not in the circumstances possible or practicable, an estimate (as near as may be) of the charges, or
>
> c. Where the provision of particulars of the actual charges or an estimate of such charges is not in the circumstances possible or practicable, the basis on which the charges are to be made...'

Conveyancing and probate should be simple and straightforward, but the cost of a court attendance varies depending on the nature of the case. The solicitor may need to attend the Garda station to obtain a report, prepare witness statements and/or consult with a barrister on your behalf.

2. Choose a Solicitor with Expertise Relevant to Your Requirements

If, for example, you need to sign a 100-page corporate lease, then employing a solicitor who specialises in family law is not such a good move as it may take him or her hours to familiarise themselves with the document, and this can prove very expensive for you. On the other hand, the solicitor skilled in this area will be familiar with the documentation and he/she will deal with it quickly.

The economic climate of today is in stark contrast to that before the recession, and it has forced many legal eagles to fly in unfamiliar territory. For example, a solicitor who specialised in conveyancing during the property boom, when he or she had likely a surplus of clients and properties to deal with, can now find him or herself accepting any work, regardless of the nature, in the absence of property to conveyance. Many solicitors are contracting the work out, loosely termed agency work in the profession, and some are registering on the Free Legal Aid panel.

3. How to Choose an Appropriate Solicitor

What area of expertise do you need? Decide, and proceed to seek recommendations from friends and colleagues about solicitors they have employed in similar circumstances. Choose a solicitor working in reasonably close proximity to your home or workplace to facilitate attending appointments.

Should you find yourself with a summons to a court sitting in a different county, contact the court and request the names of solicitors who appear there regularly (do not ask the local Gardaí as they are prosecuting you and on the opposite side). In this case, having your own solicitor present at a long-distance hearing would cost astronomically, whereas a solicitor operating locally will be substantially cheaper. Do contact the Gardaí on receiving the summons and apologise if you are pleading guilty.

4. Representing Yourself in Court

The truth is that it is not always necessary to have your solicitor with you in court if your offence is a minor one, like, for example, being found on a premises after hours, not having a TV or dog licence, speeding, driving without tax or insurance, or being unable to produce documentation. As long as you appear in court punctually and neatly dressed, and you are respectful and show remorse to the presiding judge, you can represent yourself. Have the money with you to pay any penalty fines there and then.

5. Free Legal Aid

If you cannot afford to hire a solicitor privately, you can apply for free legal aid. There are two kinds: civil legal aid and criminal legal aid.

The nature of your offence and your financial circumstances determine whether you qualify for free legal aid in the situation of a criminal offence. These cases normally start out in the District Court when the judge will decide to grant legal aid or not. Should you qualify for free legal aid, a solicitor will be appointed on your behalf.

The website www.citzensinformation.ie contains a comprehensive guide to criteria for qualifying for both types.

6. Preparation is Key

Prior to your initial meeting with your appointed solicitor, document clearly your situation, requirement(s) and your required outcome. This strategy cuts down the amount of time in the meeting substantially, as the solicitor can read through this documentation fairly quickly and he or she is not required to hear your story and take copious notes. Complete Form 1 (below), photo-copy it and bring it with you to the meeting.

7. Communication – Help Your Solicitor to Help You

Following the initial instruction, communicate any concerns by email preferably, or fax. This method of communication is fast and effective, and enables the solicitor to deal with any concerns at his or her convenience. This strategy dispenses with making numerous phone calls and follow-up appointments.

It is crucial that you communicate with your solicitor honestly, directly, clearly and using as much detail as you can. Having agreed the necessary steps with your solicitor, clarify who will deal with each task.

In your dealings with your solicitor, the area of communication is one where most of your time and your money can be spent. With a crystal clear picture in his or her mind of your situation, your solicitor can best represent you.

How well you prepare yourself prior to the meeting can also make or break your case in court. For example, perhaps you have a personal injuries claim (whiplash from a car accident) scheduled for court shortly. All medical assessments and reports from doctors appointed on both sides have been examined. If you tell your solicitor about a knee complaint not previously mentioned in your meetings with him or her, it is sure to cause anxiety prior to your court appearance.

8. Saving on Conveyancing

Regarding buying a property, it is best that you appoint your engineer and surveyor yourself, and that you deal with any loan institution or auctioneer to the point where deposits need to change hands, contracts need signing, and the property needs to be registered in your name.

This strategy dispenses with the need for excessive paperwork from your solicitor to the bank, engineer or any other, and cuts the legal costs for you. Complete Form 2 (below) for conveyancing.

In terms of selling a property, shop around for the auctioneer with the best reputation and lowest commission fee, and compare advertising costs. The website www.myhome.ie is excellent for advertising your property for sale (or for rent) with or without an auctioneer.

You can sell your property yourself by appointment only, but be safety aware and ensure that you obtain the names, addresses and telephone numbers of perspective buyers. Insist on photo ID, and show the property with friends. If you have any doubts about the identity of viewers, contact your local Garda station with names prior to the viewing.

You can potentially save a substantial amount in commission fees in selling your property yourself.

9. Renting a Home

Whether you are the landlord or the tenant, photograph the property and any contents inside and out extensively. This strategy alone will save you the cost of a lengthy legal process, and your deposit, in the event of any alleged damage to property at the end of the lease period.

Post your solicitor the photographs and the lease agreement, with a cover note detailing any concerns or proposed additions or amendments to the lease prior to signing. This dispenses with a meeting at this point. Request that you are posted a copy of the lease when it is ready for signing and proceed when you are happy with the content. You do not need your solicitor to witness this.

10. Fines and Motor Traffic Offences

Pay all fines within the 28-day period, as failure to comply within the time allotted increases the penalty amount by 50 per cent, to be paid within a further 28 days. Failure to comply leads to a court summons.

For example, the penalties for driving at a speed higher than the national speed limit are a €80 fine and two penalty points on your driving licence. Failure to pay within 28 days increases this to €120, payable within a further 28 days. If you still do not comply, you will be sent a court summons and will be subject to an increased fine and a further two penalty points.

11. Making a Will

The cost of making a will through your solicitor can range from €60 to €1,000, depending on the extent of your estate and complexity of your wishes. A recent online development in the form of an app for the iPhone, called simply iWill, guides you through the process of making a will with the help of an easy-to-read glossary of terms. It involves downloading a form, completing it and clicking on the 'Submit' button. Your will is then emailed back to you ready to execute. The cost is between €5 and €10. You can also buy a draft hardcopy template from your local stationery shop for a couple of euros. Just remember that, in order for your will to be valid, it must be signed and witnessed by two independent people (section 78, Succession Act 1965).

The above application or the hardcopy template can serve as a means of organising your thoughts before you meet your solicitor, should you decide to proceed down the traditional route.

It is far better to have it all documented prior to the meeting with your solicitor rather than to be in the meeting for endless minutes (and euros!), outlining your estate and personal belongings and who you wish to bequeath to.

Document your wishes for burial or cremation, traditional wake or funeral home, place of burial and even ceremonial details like readings, psalms and music. Remember, your loved ones are going to be grief stricken and you can make the whole process easier for them by eliminating grounds for dispute.

12. Separation or Divorce

Sadly, if you find yourself in the situation of marital breakdown, you are faced with an emotional and a financial upheaval. The legal bill, if both parties are in agreement on the terms of their separation or divorce, can be anything from €5,000 to €10,000.

When both parties are in dispute about aspects relating to access, custody, property, debts, assets and maintenance, and letters are flying to and fro through solicitors, this cost can escalate to €50,000.

Try to come to agreement with your partner on as many aspects as possible, in as much detail as you can, prior to appointing a solicitor.

If you are in an acrimonious separation, where communication has broken down, you can use a mediation service to take you to the point of agreement, when you can then legalise the terms of your agreement. You can access mediation services on www.familymediation.ie. Mediation is free from the Department of Social Protection (see www.citizensinformation.ie).

If you go the mediation route, it can help to have everything clear in your own mind, so filling out Form 3 (below) could help in that regard.

FORM 1 – Fill in Prior to Your Visit to a Solicitor

Name:
Address:

Phone:
Fax:
Email:
Nature of Business:

Requirement/Desired Outcome:

FORM 2 – Conveyancing

Full Name(s):
Address:

Date of Birth:
PPS Number:
Passport Number:
Address of Property:
Loan Institution/Broker:
Phone:
Email:
Freehold/Leasehold Address:

Description of Property/Brochure/Whereabouts of Deeds:

Price on Sale Agreed:

Auctioneer/Estate Agent
Name:
Commission Fee (%):
Address:

Phone:
Fax:
Email:
Advertising Fee:

Surveyor
Name:
Address:

Phone:
Fax:
Email:

Building Energy Regulator
Name:
Address:

Phone:
Fax:
Email:

FORM 3 – Divorce/Separation

You   *Your Partner*

Full Name: Full name:
Address: Address:

Phone: Phone:
Email: Email:
Annual Income/   Annual Income/
  Benefits: Benefits:
Occupation: Occupation:

Solicitor
Address:
Phone/Fax:
Email:

Date of Marriage:
Place of Marriage:

Children
1. Name: Age: DoB:
2. Name: Age: DoB:
3. Name: Age: DoB:
4. Name: Age: DoB:

Pets

Debt and Assets
Property Type and Estimated Value:
Mortgage Amount Outstanding:
Equity:
Debts/Outstanding Loans:
Estimated Worth of Vehicles:
Savings/Assets:
List all House and Garage Contents and Leisure
  Equipment:

My Requirements:

Describe briefly the relationship, events leading to
the deterioration of the relationship and the state
of affairs today: